HOLIDAYS, HISTORY, AND HALAKHAH

HOLIDAYS, HISTORY, AND HALAKHAH

ELIEZER SEGAL

JASON ARONSON INC.
Northvale, New Jersey
Jerusalem

This book was set in 12 pt. New Aster by Alpha Graphics of Pittsfield, NH, and printed and bound by Book-Mart Press, Inc. of North Bergen, NJ.

Library of Congress Cataloging-in-Publication Data

Segal, Eliezer.
  Holidays, history, and Halakhah / Eliezer Segal.
    p. cm.
  Includes bibliographical references and index.
  ISBN 0–7657–6151—3
  1. Fasts and feasts—Judaism. 2. Calendar, Jewish. I. Title.

BM690 S418 2000
296.4'3—dc21   00-038971

Printed in the United States of America on acid-free paper. For information and catalog write to Jason Aronson Inc., 230 Livingston Street, Northvale, NJ 07647-1726, or visit our website: www.aronson.com

Contents

Introduction   ix

THE SABBATH

Is Tsholent the Ultimate Jewish Food?   3
Why Do We Light Two Candles on Shabbat?   6
Why Do We Invite Angels to the Shabbat Table?   9

ROSH HASHANAH

Why Is Rosh Hashanah Like a Courtroom Trial?   15
Where Are We Casting Those Sins?   20
What Are the Origins of Synagogue Poetry?   23
How Did the Canadian Pioneers Assemble
  a Minyan for the Holidays?   26
What Year Is It Today?   29

YOM KIPPUR

Is There an Islamic Yom Kippur?   37
Why Has the Kol Nidré Been So Controversial?   42

What Was Wrong with the Repentance of
the Ninevites? 45
How Have People Been Transformed
by Yom Kippur? 48

SUKKOT

How Did *Hosanna* Become an English Word? 55
What Happens in the Hoshana Rabbah Moonlight? 58
How Rowdy Can It Get on Simhat Torah? 61

HANUKKAH

How Did the Maccabees Become Christian Martyrs? 67
What Is the Spiritual Aura of Hanukkah? 71
What Is Hellenism? 74
Why Is Hanukkah Considered a Women's Holiday? 77
Was Judah a "Hammerhead"? 80
What Became of the Maccabees' Menorah? 83
What Is the Origin of *Hanukkah-Gelt*? 87
Where Is the Tomb of the Last Hasmonean? 90
Why Did the Menorah Offend the Magi? 94

WINTER

What Is the Proper Date to Pray for Rain? 101

FIFTEENTH OF SHEVAT

Who Is the Incredible Plant-Man? 107

Purim

How Did Purim Turn into a Carnival?   115

Why Was There a War against Purim?   120

Was Vashti a Feminist Heroine?   124

Was Esther the First Marrano?   127

Is the Purim Story an Astrological Myth?   131

Nisan

What Is Special about the Month of Nisan?   137

Passover

Why Is the Seder Like a Roman Banquet?   143

What Is the Spiritual Symbolism of the Exodus?   147

How Does Passover Celebrate Freedom?   151

What Is the Significance of the Had Gadya?   153

Why Does Elijah Visit the Seder?   156

Why Did American Jews Drink Raisin-Wine
    on Passover?   159

Who is an "Important" Woman?   163

Why Did Some Jews Dread Passover?   166

Who Staged the First Biblical Epic?   169

Why is the Reed Sea Red?   173

The Omer Season

Why Was Judaism Split over the Counting of
    the Omer?   179

Why Do We Mourn during the Omer Season?   185

Israeli Independence Day

Were There Really Two Thousand Years of Exile?   191

Jerusalem Reunification Day

Can a Palestinian Folktale Become a Midrash?   199

Shavu'ot

Who Was Obadiah the Proselyte?   205

What Was the Shavu'ot Divorce Controversy?   208

Why Do We Decorate the Synagogue with
    Greenery on Shavu'ot?   212

What Does the *Akdamut* Teach Us about
    Ashkenazic Origins?   215

Calendrical Curiosities

What Does the Talmud Say about January 1?   221

Is There a Jewish Mother's Day?   225

Is Columbus Day a Jewish Holiday?   228

For Further Reading   231

Original Publication   245

Introduction

Nothing, it would seem, is as constant as the rhythm of the Hebrew calendar. Each year spreads before us its crop of annual holy days through which we celebrate the cycles of nature and relive the formative events in our sacred history.

The laws and customs that make up these holidays testify to the unchanging unity of Judaism—at least so it would seem when looked at on the surface.

However, as we delve deeper into the sources, and trace the traditions ever farther back through their historical evolutions, we are astonished at how much *has* changed, at how every familiar detail of the festival observances is in reality the result of a long and complex process of development. Whether we are speaking of the welcoming of angels to a Shabbat meal, the recitation of Kol Nidré on Yom Kippur, Purim masquerades or leaning at the seder table on Passover, there is scarcely a practice that was not once the topic of a controversy or variation among the various Jewish ideologies or ethnic communities. Some of our most beloved and distinctive holiday customs were borrowed from surrounding cultures, while others were adopted and reinterpreted by rival faith communities. As with so many other areas in Jewish tradition, the festival calendar bears witness to a rich and endearing diversity. Viewed from a broader historical perspective, we can appreciate that the familiar Jewish holiday customs have served as a vehicle of spiritual expression for many different ideologies and attitudes: priestly and prophetic, rationalist and mystic, pietistic and legalistic. There is scarcely a single occasion in the sacred year that does not provide us with glimpses into the fascinating variety of the tradition, while underscoring the similarities that unite our personalities and situations with those of our ancestors.

Such are the topics that are dealt with in the present collection. It is based largely on columns that I have contributed during a period of more than a dozen years for Jewish newspapers in Calgary, first the *Jewish Star*, and currently the *Jewish Free Press*. Over the years I have striven to provide an article for each approaching holiday, a challenge that has proven surprisingly easy to achieve in spite of my determination not to repeat myself from year to year. As is true of my other columns, I have benefited from the exciting new discoveries that are constantly taking place in the academic study of Judaism, discoveries that unfortunately have not been adequately appreciated outside the walls of universities and research institutes. I believe that the spiritual vigor that emerges from these sources provides a more sympathetic picture of Judaism than the anemic piety that fills the pages of so many conventional introductions to Jewish tradition.

When I first began publishing articles for a non-specialist audience, I was uncomfortable about abandoning the familiar scholarly apparatus of detailed footnotes and dry qualifications. The concept of "popular scholarship" is one that awakens suspicions among academics, who point with justifiable disdain at the sensationalism and shallowness that typify the coverage of scholarly and scientific matters in the popular media.

Without denying the validity of many of those accusations, we should recognize that there is an equally formidable danger to scholarly discourse in *not* communicating the fruits of our research to a public that stands to enjoy and benefit from them. Scholarly reticence makes it easier for demagogues and charlatans to pass off their own opinions as the dictates of a tradition without fear of having their claims challenged.

It would be an exaggeration to suggest that all my journalistic efforts spring from such high-minded civic motives. In most cases, the objectives are simpler and more immediate: I wish to offer my readers simple fare that will at once educate and entertain them during idle moments on a Shabbat or festival day.

THE SABBATH

Is Tsholent the Ultimate
Jewish Food?

Invariably the expression "Jewish food" conjures up some very vivid sensory associations in all of us. Nevertheless when we really think about it, most of the dishes that are routinely referred to as "Jewish" are in actuality nothing more than adaptations of the cuisine of the various countries to which our grandparents were scattered. The recipes are of course modified to conform to the Jewish dietary laws and, in most instances, to the impoverished circumstances in which most Jews lived. But on the whole, Polish Jewish food bears a much greater resemblance to the diet of Polish gentiles than to that of a fellow Jew in Morocco or Yemen.

Having said all this, I am still prepared to concede that there is at least one culinary item that can be accurately characterized as Jewish according to the most discriminating use of the term, and that is the humble dish known to Ashkenazic Jews as "Tsholent." Unlike almost every other one of the victuals that might lay claim to that title, the Jewishness of tsholent is not just an accidental result of the fact that many Jews happen to eat it, but its very definition is determined by the requirements of Jewish religious law. Tsholent was invented by our forefathers and foremothers in order to allow them the enjoyment of a steaming hot

Sabbath meal without violating the Torah's prohibitions against cooking and the kindling of fire. To that end, methods were devised of cooking the food before the onset of the holy day and keeping the food heated overnight. One of the more difficult chapters of the Talmud deals with the precisely defined borderlines between maintaining the heat (which is permitted) and cooking the food (which is strictly prohibited). The immense variety of formulas that ingenious Jewish cooks have invented to achieve this objective will of course vary with the available ingredients and changing tastes. The resulting dishes will also go by a broad assortment of different names. But all of them share a single halakhic definition—and what can be more uniquely Jewish than a food that is defined by Halakhah!

The very name *tsholent* attests to its quintessential Jewishness. Unlike most of the vocabulary of Ashkenazic Jewry, the name cannot be traced to either the German, Hebrew, or Slavic components of the Yiddish vernacular. Linguists are not entirely certain, but the prevailing view is that the word hearkens back to the medieval French word for heat (related to the modern French *chaleur*), testifying to the earliest stages in the migrations of the Jews who would later settle in central and Eastern Europe.

As often happens, the clearest acknowledgment of tsholent's distinctive Jewishness comes not from Jewish sources, but from the observations of outsiders. I will confine myself here to two examples: First, the Spanish Inquisition would periodically issue "Edicts of Faith" containing helpful signs through which to recognize those *conversos* who were illicitly persisting in the observance of Jewish practices. One such edict includes among these telltale acts "cooking on Fridays such food as is required for the Saturday, and on the latter eating the meat thus cooked on the Friday, as is the manner of the Jews." The preparation and consumption of tsholent thereby became declarations of Judaism for which people might face the Inquisitor's fires.

Second, travelling back in time more than a thousand years earlier, we find the Roman satirist Juvenal furnishing us with a most surprising glimpse of Jewish daily life in antiquity. In his quest for a familiar visual image that would graphically depict Jewish poverty, Juvenal makes a curious reference to those Jews whose entire material estate consists of "a basket and a box of hay." What might sound puzzling to us was quite clear to Juvenal's ancient commentators: Even the poorest of Jews were popularly known to keep a "box of hay" in which they would insulate their tsholent on Shabbat, to keep it from losing its heat, a method that is amply documented in the Mishnah and Talmud.

Thus we see that throughout our history, this humble and much-maligned steaming pot of beans and roast meat (or whatever ingredients you might happen to prefer) has been acknowledged by friend and by foe alike as a sublime expression of Jewish identity.

Why Do We Light Two Candles on Shabbat?

The lighting of the Shabbat candles on Friday evenings can be one of the most moving spiritual experiences of Jewish life, and it is not surprising that it continues to enjoy widespread popularity even among those who have few other connections to traditional Jewish observance.

The original function of Shabbat candles, as enjoined by talmudic law, was a more practical one. They were intended to enhance the enjoyment of the day by improving visibility. The sages realized that the domestic peace (*shalom bayit*) appropriate to the holy day would be diminished if members of the household were constantly stumbling over one another in the darkness.

Given this prosaic rationale, some of the familiar features of the candle-lighting ceremony are not immediately understandable. In particular, what is the significance of the *number* of candles that are kindled? I have never seen anyone light fewer than two candles, and many customs have increased the numbers—to seven, or the number of one's children, etc. Some even insist on permanently adding candles to make up for occasions when they neglected to light.

The practice of lighting two Shabbat candles was first recorded in the twelfth century, among Ashkenazic Jews,

6

and it was not adopted by their Sepharadic coreligionists until quite recently.

A popular symbolic explanation for the practice links it to variations in the wording of the Sabbath commandment that is included in the Decalogue: In Exodus we are told to *"Remember* the Sabbath day," while in Deuteronomy it says to *"Observe"* it.

Rabbinic discussions focus on more technical aspects of the practice. Several of them remark that the introduction of the second candle was intended to emphasize its special ritual dimension, to make it clear that the candles are not merely intended to provide physical illumination.

Several authorities go so far as to compare the second candle with the Hanukkah *shamash*, the role of which is to make sure that members of the household do not actually derive any benefit from the obligatory candles, which have been devoted to a sacred purpose. Toward this end, a custom existed of making the extra candle out of tallows that were legally unfit for Shabbat use.

This last point is very surprising, since the halakhic functions of Shabbat and Hanukkah candles are really quite opposite, with the former being explicitly designated for use and enjoyment, as outlined above. Nevertheless, the unanimous testimony of medieval Ashkenazic sources demonstrates that, in the popular perception, Shabbat candles were to be set aside in a holiness that precluded the deriving of benefit from them.

It is probable that the origins of this novel perception have their roots in the geographical realities of central European Jewry.

As we Calgarians will readily appreciate, summer days in northern climes can be very long. Our medieval ancestors usually adapted themselves to this situation, as most of us do, by following the halakhic option of adding to the Shabbat and ushering it in several hours before sunset.

This led to a situation in which candles were often kindled in the middle of the afternoon, when they did not provide any visible illumination. If their purpose was not a practical one—so people reasoned—then it must be a sacred and spiritual one. Eventually this attitude was translated into an actual prohibition against benefiting from their light.

Medieval rabbinic literature deals with several issues that arose from this ritualizing of the Shabbat candles. For example, it became common to light them inside the house (or in the synagogue) and then eat dinner outside in the courtyard, or for the candles to burn out long before dark. In either of these instances, the presence of the candles served no practical purpose.

Jews living in southern latitudes continued for much longer to hold on to the original understanding of the candles as an enhancement to the Sabbath's enjoyment and domestic harmony.

At any rate, the spiritualization of the Shabbat lights has by now become an inseparable part of the day's atmosphere, imbuing Jewish households with a unique glow of peace and sanctity.

Why Do We Invite Angels to the Shabbat Table?

There is a natural human need to give visual expression to abstract ideas. Toward that end people draw upon a variety of sources of inspiration.

For some of us, religious imagery is defined by the illustrations in our old schoolbooks, while others invoke great masterpieces of painting and sculpture. As for myself, my own perceptions have been decisively shaped by the cartoons I used to watch as a child.

The eternal struggle of the *Yetzer ha-tov* and the *Yetzer ha-ra*—the good and evil urges that compete within each of us—will always appear in my imagination like the little angel and imp who hover over the shoulders of animated characters pleading their respective cases.

The good and bad angels figure in several rabbinic legends. The Talmud tells how they visit Jewish homes on Friday night. If they find the household at peace and everything prepared for Shabbat, then the good angel blesses the family with the assurance that subsequent Sabbaths will be as delightful, while the bad angel reluctantly adds his "amen." But if the home is found to be in confusion and disarray, it is the bad angel's turn to wish upon the unfortunate family more unpleasant Sabbaths in the future—to which the good angel must add his unwilling assent.

The image of the angelic guests is a charming one. It is
of course the inspiration for the *Shalom Aleikhem* hymn
chanted in many Jewish homes before the Friday night meal.
In this song we greet the celestial visitors, ask for their
blessing—presumably we will be found worthy of the "good
angel's" version—and then bid our farewells as they return
to the "King of Kings of Kings" (a title that was probably
coined in antiquity in order to assert God's superiority over
the Persian monarch, who proudly called himself—as did
the Iranian Shahs in our own times—the "King of kings").

It is hard to imagine anything more beautiful, or unobjectionable, than the themes evoked by the *Shalom Aleikhem*.
It might therefore come as a surprise to learn that it became
a topic of heated controversy from its first appearance in
1641 in a prayer book printed in Prague.

The rabbis of the time had severe misgivings about the
Shalom Aleikhem. The eighteenth-century Rabbi Jacob Emden was suspicious of any mystical innovations in the traditional prayer book, because so many of them had been introduced by the supporters of the messianic pretender Shabbetai
Zvi. There were additional halakhic considerations to keep
in mind, such as the prohibition against petitionary prayers
on the Sabbath, and the fear that people might be induced
to manipulate their lamps in order to read unfamiliar supple-
ments to the *Siddur*.

Emden, as well as several other distinguished rabbinical authorities, were especially upset that a prayer was being
directed to angels, and not to the Almighty himself. After all,
Judaism had always insisted that worshippers address their
Creator directly, and often criticized the Christian reliance
on intermediaries. And yet here we are instructed to ask the
angelic emissaries for their blessing of peace.

A further objection was raised by the renowned Lithuanian scholar Rabbi Hayyim of Volozhin (1749–1821): To sup-

pose that angels can respond to our petitions implies a gross misunderstanding of their nature. According to rationalist belief, angels are mere automatons programmed to carry out specific Divine missions. They do not have the judgment or freedom of choice that would be required to comply with the human supplication for a favourable blessing.

It was in response to charges of this kind that several prayer books inserted, immediately after the *Shalom Aleikhem*, two verses from Psalms that state unmistakably that it is God who commands the angels, and protects us in our comings and goings.

Some authorities were upset by an apparent breach of supernatural etiquette. After all, as we sing the *Shalom Aleikhem* before Kiddush we seem to be hustling the angels in, asking them for their blessing and then hastily sending them on their way before the meal has even begun! Is this the proper hospitality to show to supernatural guests? Although some commentators insisted that we are not ordering the angels to depart *immediately*, not everybody was convinced.

An interesting variation on the above theme is found in a note to a prayer book published in 1880 in Lublin: "In cases of domestic disputes, refrain from singing the stanza 'Depart in peace.' According to a noted rabbi, this is a certified effective way to soothe the tensions."

Indeed, who would be so rude as to keep on quarreling when there are angels at the table?

ROSH HASHANAH

Why Is Rosh Hashanah
Like a Courtroom Trial?

The portrayal of Rosh Hashanah as a "Day of Judgment" dominates the liturgy and customs of the holiday season. As the tradition perceives it, between the New Year and the Day of Atonement God sits in judgment over all mankind to determine our fates for the coming year.

This symbolism is drawn upon to great effect by the authors of the *piyyutim*, the liturgical poems composed to enhance the statutory prayers of the season. The Jewish people, alongside the rest of humanity, are depicted as standing in a divine court-room, pleading for mercy.

If judged according to the merits of our case, we all deserve punishment. Our only hope is to persuade God to suspend the laws, or to remind him of outstanding favors owed to our forefathers.

In describing the atmosphere of the court, the rabbis and poets based themselves upon settings that were familiar to them. The courtroom is of course a well-trodden venue of talmudic Judaism and provides a wealth of details that can be elaborated in sermons and *piyyutim*.

NO LAWYERS

It is therefore most surprising to find that the court scenes that appear so prominently in rabbinic midrash and prayers as models for God's judgment of mankind are, for the most part (for reasons that are not entirely evident to me), not Jewish courts at all, but Hellenistic and Roman ones.

This fact becomes clear when we look at some of the procedural terms that are mentioned. In many of the texts, we read of debates between a *sanegor* and a *kategor*—a prosecuting and defending attorney. These are none other than the *synegoros* and *kategoros* of the Hellenistic judicial system.

In our sources the position of *kategor* is often filled by angels, who are believed to hold a mild grudge against the Jews for usurping God's special favors. The job of *sanegor* is likely to be held by the Hebrew Patriarchs, by personified representations of the "Congregation of Israel," by a person's virtuous deeds, and so forth.

Thus, in a well-known talmudic discussion, the rabbis explain why a *shofar* cannot be fashioned from a cow's horn because "the *kategor* cannot serve as *sanegor*." That is to say, the cow's horn, which holds incriminating associations with the Israelites' worship of the Golden Calf, cannot properly perform its designated function of arguing the Jews' case before the divine tribunal.

Actually, the traditional Jewish court does not permit the use of lawyers at all (though the office of "rabbinic pleader" has developed in recent years in Israel). The talmudic sources, which were familiar with the Roman court system and its susceptibility to persuasion by mellifluous rhetoric, warned the rabbis, "Do not act like the professional pleaders" (*orkhei hadayyanim*). It was the judge's job to get at the truth without its being packaged by a professional.

Nevertheless, one of the favorite High Holy Days hymns uses the same expression to designate God himself as *El Orekh Din*—the God who presides over judgment.

MILITARY METAPHORS

The Mishnah also resorts to imagery taken from Roman military life when it compares God's judgment of humankind to a commander reviewing his troops: "All the denizens of the world pass before him like a *numeron* (regiment)."

The terminology, taken from the vocabulary of the Roman legions, was unfamiliar to some of the rabbis of the Babylonian Talmud, who took it to refer to a flock of sheep being counted by the shepherd. In this version, it entered the haunting poetry of the *"Untanneh Tokef"* prayer.

A conventional sign of a victorious soldier was his return bearing in his hand a *baian*, a palm frond. The midrash saw in this Roman custom a fitting analogy to the Jewish taking of the *lulav* on Sukkot, a few days after the judgment of Yom Kippur: "Consider two parties who go to trial before a king, and no one but the king himself knows which was declared victorious. In the end, it is evident that the one who emerges holding the *baian* was the victor."

Another version of this passage uses the metaphor of a triumphant chariot racer being decorated with a wreath. So too, Sukkot is a celebration of our favourable judgment on Rosh Hashanah and Yom Kippur.

JUSTICE AND MERCY

By building upon the imagery of the Roman judicial system the midrash was able to contrast imperfect human justice with the ideal of God's judgment.

On the one hand, unlike a mortal judge, God is not subject to error, corruption, or bribery. But on the other hand, unlike most worldly judges, God's justice has the advantage of being tempered by compassion. The human being can implore God not to decree according to the standard of law, but to temper His decision with the measure of mercy.

In later *midrashim* the qualities of divine justice and mercy were no longer depicted as merely ways in which God judged His creatures, but were transformed into personalities in their own right, fulfilling the roles of *kategor* and *sanegor* in the celestial court, supplying God respectively with reasons for condemning or acquitting His creatures.

GOD ON TRIAL

A feature that has typified Jews' relationships to God from as far back as Abraham and Moses is that God can be argued with and persuaded to change His mind.

The *selichot* petitionary prayers recited at this time of year, in addition to expressing a contrite recognition of our sinfulness and powerlessness before God's will, are often characterized by an aggressive "bargaining" posture. The authors "remind" God of the suffering to which we have been subjected and of the merits earned by our righteous ancestors, and ask that these factors be counted to our credit.

This pious familiarity before God, who is perceived not only as a judge but also as a patient and forgiving father, was taken to extremes by the famous hasidic master Rabbi Levi Yitzhak of Berditchev.

Known as the "*Sanegor* of Israel" for his insistence on always seeing his fellow Jews in a favourable light, Levi Yitzhak is said to have challenged God one Rosh Hashanah to a lawsuit—a *din Torah*. God, he argued, had no right to prolong Israel's exile when other more sinful nations were allowed to live in peace and prosperity.

A grim variation on this story is recounted by Elie Wiesel in his Holocaust memoir *Night*, and later formed the basis for his play "The Trial of God." On Rosh Hashanah, from the depths of their sorrow and despair, the inmates of Auschwitz called God to judgment and condemned him for allowing such evil and suffering in His world.

Both stories, that of Levi Yitzhak of Berditchev and that of the Auschwitz inmates, end in the same way. After declaring God's guilt the accusers rise to recite the *Kaddish*— the proclamation of God's sovereignty over the universe.

The point is a profound one: For the Jew, it is possible to argue against God, but not to live without Him.

May all our judgments during the coming year be favorable ones.

Where Are We Casting Those Sins?

Rosh Hashanah suffers from no lack of diverse prayers, laws, and customs. I personally have a special fondness for the *Tashlikh* ceremony. Taking a brief respite from the long hours in synagogue and around the table, the community gathers in the afternoon at the Glenmore reservoir to enjoy some fresh air and to metaphorically divest ourselves of our sins. The widespread practice in most communities today is to turn one's pockets inside-out, jettisoning some lint or, at most, a few crumbs that might be taken along for the occasion. The ceremony is symbolic of our determination to free ourselves from our sins and shortcomings during this special season.

The ritual of *Tashlikh* is not mentioned in either the Bible or the Talmud, and yet its origins are believed to go back to antiquity. Perhaps the earliest reference to it is preserved in a passage from Rashi's commentary to the Babylonian Talmud. In explaining an obscure talmudic word *parpisa*, Rashi, basing himself on the writings of the Babylonian *Ge'onim*, describes a custom of filling baskets with beans during the weeks before Rosh Hashanah, rotating them over the heads of each family member to "absorb" their transgressions, and then casting the baskets into the sea. The practice, a variant on the familiar *kapparot* rite, indicates that the origins of the two customs are probably very close. Some scholars have connected the word *parpisa* with the Latin *propitio*, or propitiation.

As we have noted, current custom does not attach too much emphasis to the objects that are to be cast into the waters, nor for that matter to the precise bodies of water that are to be visited. Subject to availability, I have seen *Tashlikh* performed at anything from a beach to a well to a bathtub. The residents of Safed would stand on their rooftops facing the Sea of Galilee, whereas the Kurdish Jews did not feel suitably purified unless they actually jumped into the river.

Medieval writings present a decidedly different picture of the folk practice. In the popular consciousness it was crucial to bring along substantial quantities of foodstuffs, and some insisted on going directly from the dinner table with the remains of the festive meal. It was equally important to go to a body of water with visible fish, so that one could actively feed them. Watching the fish was perceived as an important element in the ceremony.

This concern for the precise fate or destination of the food does not seem relevant if our desire is merely to rid ourselves of our sins. Some modern scholars have therefore suggested, with some justification, that the original practice had a different purpose, that of buying off the forces of evil whose abode was believed to lie in the depths of the sea and to whom the fish would eventually carry these "offerings." In this connection, several medieval authorities cite the midrashic tradition of how Satan took the guise of a river in order to prevent Abraham from sacrificing Isaac.

However, most rabbis were scrupulous to avoid such mythic or superstitious explanations of the *Tashlikh* ritual, and discouraged the practices with which they were associated, particularly those which gave the appearance of feeding the demonic forces. They preferred to emphasize more orthodox motifs, like the casting away of sins, or of beholding God's greatness in the vastness of the sea. Several commentators dwell on the symbolism of the fish. Like the Almighty, their eyes never close. Like man, they are ever vulnerable to death's inexorable net.

As with much of Jewish practice, our tradition has provided us with powerful symbols that can be interpreted in an infinite variety of ways, and can therefore effectively convey their message to the hearts and minds of each and every one of us.

What Are the Origins
of Synagogue Poetry?

O ne of the many features that contribute to the unique-
ness of the New Year's season is the abundance of poetic
additions to the standard prayers. These passages are known
in Hebrew as *piyyut*, from the same Greek root that gives us
the English words "poetry" and "poet."

Although in our synagogues the recitation of *piyyutim*
has become almost the exclusive prerogative of the High
Holy Days, many communities include them on other special occasions as well. The term *Mahzor*, which we usually
associate only with *Rosh Hashanah* and *Yom Kippur*, actually translates as "cycle," and originally included prayers—
primarily the poetic elaborations—for the entire year, especially the holidays.

Our knowledge about the purpose and history of *piyyut*
has been immeasurably enriched by manuscript discoveries over the last century, especially from the Cairo *Genizah*.
The *Genizah* preserved thousands of poetic creations, and
the analysis and appreciation of those works has become one
of the most exciting areas of recent Judaic scholarship.

From this new evidence we have been able to paint a
vivid picture of how central *piyyut* was to synagogue life in
the Land of Israel during the talmudic and early medieval
eras. It was on native soil that this art form thrived. The

ancient rabbis encouraged innovation and improvisation in public worship to counterbalance the mechanical recitation of fixed texts. In keeping with these sentiments, the original *piyyutim* did not appear as additions or embellishments to the fixed liturgy—as they do in our rites—but as replacements for them.

Indeed, the prolific cantors of old were able to compose original poetic versions of the prayers for each and every Shabbat, as well as for the festivals. In those *piyyutim* the motifs of the *Shema* and *Amidah* would be ingeniously meshed with topics from the day's Torah and *haftarah* readings.

This was no small achievement if we recall that in ancient Israel the reading of the Torah was not completed in a single year as it is now, but in three and a half years. Thus a *payyetan* might have to compose a *Mahzor* of almost two hundred different renderings of the Shabbat and holiday services before he could revert back to old material.

The complexity and erudition of classical *piyyut* is utterly astounding. To take as an example the renowned poet Yannai, we note that he specialized in a particular type of *piyyut* known as the *Kedushta*, which gave poetic form to the first three blessings of the *Shaharit* service for Shabbat and festival *Amidah*. (In those days the *Kedushah* was not recited outside the Morning Service.) Every one of Yannai's *Kedushta*s was composed of nine separate sections, each of which had to conform to strict formal rules that dictated the meter and number of lines and stanzas, rhyme, acrostic structures (that is, the initial letters of lines would spell out the author's name or be in alphabetical order), the incorporation of verses from the day's Torah and Prophetic readings, and so on.

Within this confining structure, Yannai and his colleagues worked their poetic magic. Their creations are stamped with masterful scholarly erudition in their frequent allusions to the full range of biblical and rabbinic literature and in the creative liberties they take with the Hebrew language. Alongside these learned and didactic qualities, the finest *piyyutim* succeed in poignantly and movingly evoking the sublime emotions of religious awe and the unrelenting longing for national redemption from the yokes of Rome and Byzantium.

During the Middle Ages, as the Babylonian rabbinate strove to assert its dominance against the Palestinian religious leadership, the use of *piyyut* came under heavy attack. The Babylonians preferred uniform and standardized rituals and were wary of the spontaneity that *piyyut* embodied. Nevertheless the ancient Palestinian tradition was kept alive, especially in the Jewish communities of France and Germany whose founders had originally migrated from the Holy Land. Many of the most illustrious Ashkenazic scholars were also accomplished poets whose creations still adorn the pages of our *Mahzor*.

Recent generations have been uneasy about the inclusion of *piyyut* in the service for various reasons. Some argue that they distract from the mandatory prayers; others complain that they unduly prolong the service, and that few Jews are now literate enough to appreciate them. Though all these arguments might have merit, it would be a pity if they were to result in the abandoning of some of our most precious literary and religious treasures.

How Did the Canadian Pioneers Assemble a *Minyan* for the Holidays?

A s our local synagogues struggle with the formidable challenges of accommodating the crowds of worshippers who converge upon them during the current High Holy Days season, it demands some effort to recall that there were times in the not so distant past when small and fragile Canadian Jewish communities faced great difficulties in their endeavors to piece together makeshift religious services for Rosh Hashanah and Yom Kippur.

As a tiny trickle of pioneering Jews first made its way to the Canadian wilds, even to the northwesterly frontiers of the new land, the convening of a *minyan* for the holidays came to have profound symbolic importance as a token of a community's permanence.

In those rugged days there were usually no special buildings set aside as houses of Jewish prayer, and the services might be held in a variety of exotic settings.

In some cases, a private home was sufficient for the purpose of High Holy Days worship. That was how things were done in Prince Rupert, British Columbia, during the community's infancy in the early decades of this century, in Winnipeg in 1879 (without the benefit of a Torah scroll), and in Victoria as far back as 1858. By 1862, Victoria's "First Hebrew Benevolent Society" was soliciting subscriptions in order to acquire a plot of land (for $730!) upon which to erect a real synagogue, a project that would be completed within a few years. The first president of the Benevolent Society was a hardware dealer and ironmonger named Abraham Blackman, who also officiated as the cantor for Kol Nidré and as treasurer of the shul upon its completion.

A simple commercial establishment also served as a synagogue for the forty participants who gathered for the 1898 Rosh Hashanah services at Dawson City in the Yukon, held in the latter days of the Klondike Gold Rush. By Yom Kippur the worshippers were able to move into the town's Yukon Pioneer Hall. Similarly, by the second year of their existence, in 1880, the Winnipeg congregation had overflowed into the Orange Hall (using a *sefer* Torah sent from Chicago), and the following year they gathered in the Oddfellow's Hall.

Though scheduling prayers in a social hall might have been an improvement over private residences and storefronts, it could also give rise to some unexpected inconveniences. Such was the fate of the dozen or so Jews who congregated for Yom Kippur prayers in Moose Jaw, Saskatchewan, in 1912. They were compelled to vacate the premises immediately after the *Minchah* service in order to make room for a dance.

Whatever latitudes they might permit themselves in their choice of venue, the fledgling congregations could hardly forego the halakhic minimum of ten adult males to make up a proper *minyan*. Understandably, the body count was not always an easy goal to accomplish.

When Jacob Diamond realized his dream of convening formal religious services in Calgary for the 1894 holiday season, he could not count on an automatic quorum of local residents. In addition to himself, his brother, William, and two other Calgarian Jews, he had to import two participants from Edmonton, a farmer from Lacombe, and five peddlers who were passing through the city at the time.

A similar predicament beset the handful of Jews in Saint John, New Brunswick, when they sought to hold New Year's services in 1879. By then the town could lay claim to eight of its very own Jewish males, a circumstance that encouraged the community's leader, Solomon Hart, to schedule public worship that year. However, completing the quorum would prove to be a more complex challenge than he had anticipated.

The ninth member of the minyan was a peddler who happened to be passing through from Montreal. Having received a commitment from him to remain in Saint John for Yom Tov, the congregation were ready to complete the quorum by inviting an American lay cantor, who also agreed to furnish the shofar and Torah scroll.

The Rosh Hashanah worship took place as scheduled. Unfortunately, the impatient Montrealer deserted from the ranks immediately afterwards, leaving the disappointed Saint John congregation with the prospect of a *minyan*-less Day of Atonement.

Local legend describes how Solomon Hart personally made the rounds of every hotel in town, scouring the guest lists for Jewish-sounding names. At the last minute he did succeed in locating a Jew from Boston who was just about to return home for the holiday. Hart implored the traveler to remain in town for the occasion.

The traveler did succumb to the entreaties, and Yom Kippur services were held in St. John that year.

For a full week afterwards, the delighted Hart continued to pour out his family's gratitude and hospitality upon this Bostonian, whom he had characterized as a veritable "Elijah the Prophet, an angel sent by God."

What Year Is It Today?

A prosaic, though important, consequence of Rosh Hashanah's status as a "new year" is the fact that it involves turning a page in the Hebrew calendar. For example, we are currently in the 5760s "from the creation of the world."

The practice of reckoning dates from the creation was apparently not known or practiced by the rabbis of the Talmud. The Mishnah discusses several options for dating legal documents, and evidently permits only those that refer to the year in the term of the reigning king. Among the non-sanctioned dating systems, the sources mention reckonings "from the building of the Temple," "from the destruction of the Temple," and some others.

From the combined testimony of the Talmud and archeological data it is evident that the Jews, like their gentile neighbors, followed the convention of identifying years by the name of the incumbent ruler. Usually this was the Roman Emperor, but it could also be the consul or the provincial eparch.

The Babylonian Talmud informs us that one dating system was in use there: "according to the kings of Greece."

The reference here is to a practice that was in widespread use in antiquity, of indicating dates from a chro-

29

nological point that is equivalent to the year 312 B.C.E. That was the year when the momentous battle at Gaza effectively divided up the Middle East between two of Alexander the Great's generals, establishing the Seleucid and Ptolemaic empires.

The political and military tensions between those two superpowers (with Judea situated precariously in the middle) defined the Middle-Eastern map for centuries afterwards, until both fell to the Romans. Modern historians designate this dating system as "the Seleucid era."

In typical fashion, the Jews held tenaciously to this ancient calendric system long after those Hellenistic kingdoms had departed from the stage of history. Similar phenomena can be adduced in the realms of language, dress, and so forth, where Jewish customs preserve practices that can no longer be found among the gentiles from whom they were originally borrowed.

Throughout the medieval era, the Seleucid system remained the only officially sanctioned manner for recording dates in legal deeds among the communities that followed the Babylonian rite, and hence it was standardly designated as *minyan ha-shetarot*, the "documentary reckoning." It was presupposed by the renowned Babylonian *Ga'on* Rabbi Sherira in his masterful chronology of rabbinic literature, and continued to be employed by Yemenite Jews well into the twentieth century.

What, then, is the origin of the practice of indicating dates from the Creation?

The literary source for this chronology is a midrashic compilation known as *Seder 'Olam* (the Order of the World) composed by the second-century sage Rabbi Yosé ben Halafta of Sepphoris. *Seder 'Olam* is explicitly devoted to the problem of calculating the sequences of events in Jewish history, based largely on the information supplied by the Bible. Even though *Seder 'Olam* studiously counts the days and years between the individual events of scriptural history, it does not actually provide the total number of years that elapsed since the creation. At any rate, it was the only work of its sort to be attempted by the ancient rabbis, and it was cited approvingly in the Talmud.

I stated above that *Seder 'Olam*'s calculations were based "largely" on the Bible. There were in fact several exceptions to this characterization, in which Rabbi Yosé made use of more imaginative midrashic interpretations that were not supported by a straightforward reading of Scripture. Some medieval chroniclers who attempted their own calculations of the "creation" date based on their reading of the biblical evidence, such as Rabbi Abraham Ibn Daud in his *Sefer Ha-Qabbalah*, reached conclusions that were at variance with those of *Seder 'Olam*.

Although Jews who were politically subject to the Baghdadi Caliphate (and hence, religiously, to the Babylonian *Ga'on*) continued to follow the talmudic convention of dating according to the "Greek kings," those communities that continued to accept the authority of the Palestinian leadership—primarily in Egypt and southern Italy, as well as the Holy Land itself—took the *Seder 'Olam* chronology as their norm in legal documents, which they dated from the alleged creation of the world. The founders of European Jewry seem to have inherited this practice from their ancestors in the Land of Israel.

For most Jews in medieval Europe, whose knowledge of history was confined to biblical and talmudic sources, the creation dates proved adequate and served them well for centuries.

Eventually the system did face a challenge. By the sixteenth century, educated Italian Jews were participating in the thriving culture of Renaissance scholarship, which included the critical study of ancient documents. Prominent among the Jewish humanists was Rabbi Azariah de Rossi of Mantua who composed a special work, the *Ma'or 'Einayim* (*Enlightenment of the Eyes*) devoted to the enrichment of Jewish historical understanding through the utilization of material preserved in Greek and Latin.

One of the many topics that was subjected to de Rossi's historical critique was the traditional calendar reckoning. Remarking that it was in any case a relatively recent convention, he meticulously demonstrated that it was also factually inaccurate. In some cases, he argued, the biblical evidence was simply not sufficient to fill in the entire chronological sequence.

The most conspicuous weaknesses of the *Seder 'Olam* system related to those eras that were not directly covered in the Bible, especially the Persian era, for which the traditional rabbinic chronology had to rely mainly on the cryptic historical allusions contained in the Book of Daniel. De Rossi showed that, when checked against the extra-biblical historical records, the resulting chronology was severely flawed, cutting the era short by some 165 years!

Although Rabbi Azariah's conclusions were irrefutably correct, they became a topic of heated controversy. Conservative rabbis were convinced that by calling into question this relatively unimportant detail from the "received tradition," the gates would be opened for a frontal assault on the foundations of Jewish faith. Some of the traditionalists tried to appeal to Rabbi Joseph Karo, author of the *Shulhan 'Arukh*, urging him to ban the book. Karo did in fact compose an order for the burning of the *Ma'or 'Einayim*, but died before it could be implemented. Nonetheless, several communities issued decrees setting strict limits on who could read the work.

Of course, matters have changed a lot since then. Now that the scientific estimates of the ages of the universe, of our planet, and of the human race, have taught us to translate these eras into mind-boggling billions of years, there are few Jews who would insist on treating those traditional numbers as anything but symbolic.

But then again, are not symbols precisely what a religious tradition is all about?

YOM KIPPUR

Is There an Islamic Yom Kippur?

While political events tend to emphasize the divisions between Jews and Muslims, for students of the Islamic past it is the uncanny similarities between the two religious traditions that continually arouse one's amazement. The resemblances extend to many areas of ritual and observance.

Muhammad, the founder of the Islamic faith, was in close contact with the affluent and influential Jewish tribes of Arabia (among whom were to be found the ancestors of today's Yemenite Jews) who probably accounted for the majority of the population of al-Madinah, the first Islamic community.

Much Jewish teaching was incorporated into Muhammad's message, and he in turn directed much of his preaching to the Jews, in hope that they would accept him as a true prophet. Almost all of the names used to designate the principal observances of Islam derive from Hebrew or Aramaic terms that were in common use among the Jews.

FAST OF RAMADAN

Many are aware that Muslims devote an entire month—that of Ramadan—to a fast that extends through the day-

light hours, in commemoration of the revelation of the
Qur'an, the sacred scripture of Islam. The fast is known as
the *sawm* (identical to the Hebrew word for a fast, *tzom*).
Less widely known is the fact that the institution of Ramadan
took the place of an earlier practice, a single-day (twenty-
four hour) fast known in Arabic as the *Ashura*.

Islamic tradition bases this custom on a reference in the
Qur'an (1:79) to keeping "the fast as it was prescribed for
those before you." Muslim tradition explains that "those
before you" were the Jews, and that Muhammad in this
passage was commanding that his followers adopt the Jewish custom of fasting on the Day of Atonement.

The Arabic word *Ashura* is none other than the Hebrew
word *Asor*, the tenth, the term used in the Bible (Leviticus
16:29, etc.) to designate the date of the holiday (the tenth
day of the seventh month).

The origin of this precept is described in the Muslim
"oral tradition" (*Hadith*) as collected by the noted ninth-
century authority, Al-Bukhari:

> When the Prophet came to al-Madinah he found
> that the Jews observed the fast of *Ashura*. He en-
> quired about this and was told that it was the day
> on which God had delivered the Children of Israel
> from the enemy and Moses used to keep a fast on
> it as an expression of gratitude to the Almighty. The
> Prophet thereupon remarked that "Moses has a
> greater claim upon me than upon you," and he
> fasted on that day and instructed his followers to
> do the same.

The reference to the deliverance from "the enemy" is puzzling. In other versions of this tradition, the event is explicitly identified as the drowning of Pharaoh's armies in the

Red Sea. This does not seem to correspond with any Jewish traditions about the significance of Yom Kippur.

JOY OF YOM KIPPUR

Muslim interpreters were further puzzled by other traditions that depicted the Jewish holiday in question as a joyous festival, in which women were accustomed to dressing up in ornamental finery. This did not seem to agree with the biblical portrayal of a solemn day devoted to contrite prayers for the atonement of sins.

Some Islamic scholars were consequently moved to reject the traditional identification, and applied it to Passover. Such an identification was made more likely by the dual system used for enumerating the Jewish months, according to which the month that had originally been counted the first (Nisan) came later to be regarded as the seventh. The fact is, however, that the older Islamic traditions do appear accurate. In a way that non-Jews often have difficulty appreciating, the Jewish mood on Yom Kippur has always been one of joy and good spirits, precisely because of the confidence that God has indeed forgiven our sins and we may joyfully begin life anew with a clean slate.

The Mishnah (end of *Ta'anit*) describes this atmosphere vividly: "Israel knew no days as joyous as . . . the Day of Atonement, in which the daughters of Jerusalem would go out in . . . white garments and dance in the vineyards. . . ."

As to the question of the supposed victory over Moses's enemy on Yom Kippur, it seems clear that the original reference was not to Pharaoh or any mortal foe of the Jews, but rather to Satan (the Hebrew term literally translates as "the Antagonist"). This accords with the traditional Jewish identification of Yom Kippur as the day on which Moses finally concluded the forty days of prayer and pleading with God to forgive the Israelites for the sin of worshipping the golden calf.

According to the Midrash, it was on Yom Kippur that God finally announced (against the counterarguments proposed by Satan) that Moses was allowed to present the people with the second tablets of the Law. This story was well known to Muhammad, and alluded to elsewhere in the Qur'an.

JEWISH ROOTS

There are a number of other instances in the development of Islamic ritual, in which Muhammad is reported to have ordered a shift away from an earlier practice that had been identical with the Jewish observance.

Such changes have normally been attributed to Muhammad's frustration at the fact that the Jews did not ultimately come to accept him as a prophet. Thus, for instance, he originally ordered that his followers pray three times a day and in the direction of Jerusalem—like the Jews—but later altered it to five times, and toward Mecca.

In the case of the *Ashura*, however, the story is somewhat different. While Muhammad did indeed replace it with the fast of Ramadan, he did not altogether abolish the former custom, and pious Muslims, especially among the Shiites (for whom the date has other historical associations), are still encouraged to observe the tenth day of the month Muharram as a voluntary fast, "to atone for the sins of the coming years."

The last ten days of Ramadan (termed *I'tikaf*) have a special status, and have been traced by scholars to the custom of some pious Jews of fasting throughout the "ten days of penitence" between Rosh Hashanah and Yom Kippur.

Medieval tradition recommends that pious Muslims also fast on Mondays and Thursdays, another custom that has venerable Jewish roots. Some scholars have even suggested that the idea of fasting for an entire month also has its root in the Jewish custom of observing the whole month of Elul as a penitential period. The association with the revelation of the Qur'an also parallels the Jewish identification of Yom Kippur with Moses' giving of the second set of tablets.

Why Has the Kol Nidré Been So Controversial?

The solemnity of the Kol Nidré ceremony is matched only by its puzzling character. Why should a legal ritual for the annulment of vows be inserted into the beginning of what is supposed to be a day of intense prayer? Why, for that matter, should vows be annulled at all? Should they not simply be fulfilled?

The institution of annulment is in itself an ancient one and is mentioned in some of the earliest passages in the Mishnah. A person, having committed him/herself to a vow, can come before a sage to be released from the vow. The release normally took the form of an interrogation whose purpose was to establish that the vow had been accepted originally without full awareness of its implications or consequences. Once it was established that the vow had been undertaken under mistaken premises, then the sage had the authority to declare it null and void.

The earliest rabbinic authorities were unclear about the origin of this institution. The Mishnah (*Hagigah* 1:8) includes it among the laws that "hover in the air and have nothing to support them"—that is, they are part of the oral tradition, with no scriptural basis. Some conflicting views recorded in the Talmud try to find biblical support for the institution through imaginative readings of several verses.

Among the medieval rabbis the status of the annulment of vows continued to be the subject of a dispute. Maimonides, while acknowledging that the institution is part of the oral law rather than a scriptural rule, enumerates it among the 613 commandments of the Torah. In order to do so he must explain that he is using the concept "commandment" in an unusual way: Not that any individual has an obligation to annul his or her vows, but rather the rabbinical court has the duty to deal with requests for annulment. Other commentators argued that this sort of rule cannot, strictly speaking, be termed a commandment, and that rabbis should be reluctant in promoting laxity in the fulfillment of religious obligations.

The existence of a Kol Nidré ceremony is first attested from the tenth century. (Contrary to a widespread theory, there is no basis for the association of the ritual with the Spanish Marranos.) The association of Kol Nidré with Yom Kippur probably reflects a popular feeling that unfulfilled obligations would impede the atonement process. The earliest versions of the ceremony are worded so as to retroactively absolve the vows of the previous year. This procedure was later modified in most rites, and changed into an annulment of *next* year's vows.

Most leading rabbinic authorities were initially hostile to this custom. They noted that the public ceremony did not conform to the normal requirements for annulment of vows, which include individual interrogation and the expression of regret. The heads of the Babylonian academies flatly refused to give sanction to what they regarded as an unjustifiable disregard for the explicit biblical precept "If a man vow unto the Lord . . . he shall not break his word" (Numbers 30:2). They even refused to study the talmudic tractates that dealt with this topic.

Over the years, however, it became more and more difficult to resist the demand from people who had recklessly gotten themselves tied into obligations that they were now unable to fulfil. The phenomenon of vows has always been associated primarily with the common people, who would use them as a way of emphasizing assertions (even as it is common in English to preface assertions with such phrases as "Damn me if . . ."). *After* the fact, the same people took their words seriously enough to be concerned that their unfulfilled vows would obstruct the efficacy of Yom Kippur.

In the end, the rabbis were compelled to make a difficult choice between insistence on respect for one's word, and compassion for those real people who urgently needed a procedure for easing their consciences and permitting their forgiveness.

The history of this very human dilemma is the story of the controversy over the Kol Nidré.

What Was Wrong with the Repentance of the Ninevites?

The choice of the Book of Jonah as the Torah reading for the Yom Kippur Afternoon Service undoubtedly stems from its universal lessons about the power of repentance.

To the prophet's exasperation, the Almighty accepted the people of Nineveh's sincere commitment to turn from their evil ways, and canceled his threat to destroy the city. Jonah himself, in his shortsighted determination to avert the rescue of Nineveh, does not come across in a very favourable light.

The ancient rabbis, especially in the Babylonian Talmud, studied the biblical description of the Ninevites' change of heart, citing it as a paradigm to be emulated by all persons who wish to repair their relationships with their Creator.

Surprisingly, in some of the ancient rabbinic works composed in the Land of Israel, we encounter a very different assessment of the events. These texts accuse the people of Nineveh of staging an elaborate deception, of feigning their repentance, and even of impudently threatening to cause suffering to innocent beasts unless God would agree to exercise compassion.

As for the people's declaration "Let every one turn from his evil way and from the iniquity which is in his hands," the midrashic sources read this in a narrowly legalistic manner: Only those ill-gotten items that were *literally* in their hands at the time did they agree to restore—but articles that were kept in chests and coffers were excluded from the commitment.

Why did the Jewish sages go to such pains to discredit the Ninevites, in blatant disregard for the apparent meaning of the Bible text?

It would appear that here, as in many similar instances, the rabbis were responding to an ideological challenge. For the repentance of Nineveh had become a focus of the fierce polemical exchanges that typified Jewish-Christian contacts during the early development of the church.

In some of the Gospels, utilizing an idea that appears in Jewish preaching as well, Jesus compares himself to Jonah, who succeeded in influencing the gentiles while failing to achieve equivalent success among his compatriots; "The men of Nineveh shall rise up in the judgment with this generation, and shall condemn it: for they repented at the preaching of Jonah."

Viewed in light of such charges, Jonah came to be depicted by the Midrash as a virtual national hero whose devotion to his people impelled him to refuse his mission in order to prevent future generations of Jews from being subjected to the unflattering contrast. In doing so, Jonah was joining a respectable line of prophets, including Moses himself, who were ready to put their own souls on the line to protect the interests of their people.

This interpretation would be repeated in the commentary of the third- and fourth-century Church Father Jerome, who lived in the Holy Land and studied extensively with Jewish teachers. Echoing the rabbinic traditions, Jerome has Jonah bemoaning his fate: "I alone was selected from among all the prophets, so that in bringing salvation to others, I shall herald the ruin of my own people."

Another Christian writer, Efrem the Syrian, told how the grateful Ninevites wanted to escort Jonah back to his homeland, but the prophet put them off, ashamed lest the heathen guests witness the sinfulness of his own people.

In a possible reaction to the strong influence of Jewish practices and ideas in the Syrian Church, Efrem did not pass up this opportunity to berate the Jews for their reliance on the merits of their forefathers, and for valuing the Law more than the God who gave it. Efrem concluded his account by having the people of Nineveh praise God "for humiliating the Jews by means of the gentiles."

The midrashic defamation of the Ninevites is therefore recorded only in sources that emanate from the Land of Israel, where Christianity was making successful inroads in the wake of the various tragedies that were besetting the Jewish nation.

It is against this background, of Christian apologists making unflattering comparisons between the sincerity of the pagans and the stubbornness of the Jews, that we ought to appreciate the rabbinic vilification of the Ninevites and their admiration for Jonah's solidarity with his people. The prophet, they felt, had foreseen the destructive uses to which his mission would one day be put by Israel's rivals.

How Have People Been Transformed by Yom Kippur?

Whether in first-century Alexandria or in contemporary Calgary, Yom Kippur—the Jewish Day of Atonement—has maintained an inexplicable hold, even over Jews who in other respects have become severed from their spiritual roots. The holiday's power is not diminished by its dearth of tangible symbols, historical associations, or links to the cycles of nature.

The following two vignettes illustrate the awesome force that can be exerted by this sacred day over Jew and Gentile alike:

> In 1911 Rudolf Otto, a young German lecturer in theology, undertook a journey to North Africa, India, and the Far East. The Day of Atonement that year found him, a Christian, in the Moroccan town of Mogador, where he visited the local synagogue. Amidst the material squalor of the setting, Otto was overwhelmed by the grandeur of the Hebrew chanting, particularly of the *Kedushah*, that sublime prayer in which the community emulates the angelic adulation of the Almighty as portrayed in the mystic visions of Isaiah and Ezekiel: "Holy, Holy, Holy is the Lord of Hosts!"

In this experience were sown the seeds of Otto's lifelong fascination with the experience of holiness in world religions. In his seminal work, *The Idea of the Holy*, he explored the essence of the "mysterium tremendum" that engulfs individuals when they stand before the power of a "wholly other" majesty that transcends rational understanding.

In Otto's analysis of the holiness experience, it is the process of atonement that allows us to bridge the chasm of profane unworthiness and enter into a relationship with God.

In another episode that occurred shortly afterwards, the spell of Yom Kippur saved Judaism from losing one of its most creative and heroic teachers:

Like many of his Jewish contemporaries in turn-of-the-century Germany, young Franz Rosenzweig embarked upon a quest for personal religious solutions to the puzzles of human existence. Though unsatisfied by the aridity of the prevailing philosophical schools, his superficial Jewish education had not equipped him to counter the attractions of liberal Protestantism, which professed to embody the essence of enlightened universalism.

In 1913 Rosenzweig resolved to adopt Christianity, a move that was conventionally viewed as a necessary prerequisite to full acceptance into European culture and society. However, he wished to enter the new religion "as a Jew," and therefore determined to spend the last days before his conversion in Jewish settings, emulating the founders of Christianity who had seen the new faith as a fulfillment of their Judaism.

When Rosenzweig confided his plans to his mother, she threatened to have her apostate son turned away from the Yom Kippur services in the central synagogue of Cassel. It thus turned out that Rosenzweig attended worship on Oct. 11, 1913, at a tiny orthodox house of prayer (*shtiebl*) in Berlin.

The experience was an overpowering one. Rosenzweig never described precisely what it was that transformed him in that Berlin synagogue, but we know that immediately afterwards his perspectives underwent a complete reversal, and that the prospect of conversion was "no longer possible."

In later writings Rosenzweig emphasized that, beyond feelings of personal exaltation and communal solidarity, Yom Kippur constitutes "a testimony to the reality of God that cannot be controverted." He described movingly how on that day every Jew "confronts the eyes of his judge in utter loneliness as if he were dead in the midst of life. . . ." And yet, in spite of the apparently unbridgable gap between individual and Creator, on Yom Kippur "he is as close to God . . . as it is ever accorded man to be."

Whatever it was that Rosenzweig experienced in that Berlin synagogue, it impelled him to devote the remainder of his life—much of it in the grip of a debilitating illness—to studying and teaching the Jewish tradition. His *Star of Redemption* remains one of the most challenging works of Jewish theology. His collaboration with Martin Buber produced a fresh new German translation of the Hebrew Bible and under his leadership the Frankfurt *Freies Jüdisches Lehrhaus* inspired some of German Jewry's most distinguished intellectuals.

Perhaps it is Yom Kippur's very defiance of historical or natural context that cries out against the facile determinisms of modern ideologies. Starkly alone before our Creator, we acknowledge that the power to change life's course belongs to no one but ourselves.

SUKKOT

How Did *Hosanna* Become an English Word?

It usually comes as no great surprise to encounter Hebrew words that have become part of the English language. In almost all such instances the word in question will be part of the vocabulary of the Hebrew Bible, which is of course a foundation document of Western civilization, revered and studied by Christians as well as by Jews.

An exceptional case is that of the English word *hosanna*, which is defined in English dictionaries as "an exclamation of praise, acclamation, or adoration." Underlying the English form is the Hebrew *hosha' na*, which expresses a request for salvation. This precise form of the expression is not actually found anywhere in the Bible, nor does its meaning fit the dictionaries' associations with praise or acclamation.

Most readers will of course recognize the word from its use in the processions that are an important part of the daily services during the Sukkot holiday. Waving our *lulavim* we circle the synagogue reciting prayers with the repeated litany of "Hosha'na," "God save us!" as we beseech God for a bounteous and rain-filled year and for a speedy national redemption. On the seventh day, known as "the Great Hoshana" (*Hoshana' Rabbah*) the ceremony is performed repeatedly and with great solemnity. The "Hosha'na" formula originated as the Aramaic rendering of the Hebrew "Hoshi'a na" in the Hallel (Psalms 118:25). The Talmud reports that in colloquial Aramaic the word became synonymous with willow branches, on account of their use in the special processions of Hoshana Rabbah, in accordance with ancient traditional practice.

The rituals described above, though central to Jewish observance, are not prescribed explicitly in the Torah, which speaks only in general terms of taking the "four species" and rejoicing before God seven days (Leviticus 23:40). How then did they become part of the English language?

The answer to this question is to be sought in Christian scriptures. The New Testament writers describe how Jesus's last entry to Jerusalem was accompanied by enthusiastic crowds shouting "Hosanna!" in expectation of the Messiah. Some versions add that the greeters were carrying palm fronds. Possibly it was precisely because the literal rendering did not fit the narrative context, where it expresses triumph rather than beseeching, that the Greek writers of the New Testament intentionally left the expression untranslated—a circumstance that made possible its eventual acceptance into English. Those of us who are familiar with rabbinic midrash will however recall that the taking of the *lulav* is indeed described there (following the Greek convention) as a gesture of victory, as the Jewish people emerges triumphant from its judgment on Rosh Hashanah and Yom Kippur.

There are several ironies and difficulties in the New Testament's description of the incident. The account seems to suppose that it took place on or around Sukkot, although the events are generally supposed to have occurred on Passover. Furthermore, we have seen that the *Hoshanna* ritual is a typical example of Jewish Oral Tradition, and not part of the Written Torah. This is precisely the kind of observance that Jesus himself would probably have rejected as an unacceptably human creation. And yet the symbolism of the procession came to occupy a central place in Christian belief and practice. (It is of course the source for the feast of Palm Sunday.)

The episode is one of many in Christian scriptures that is more likely to be appreciated by Jews than by the average Christian. Not only does it present vivid testimony to an ancient Jewish practice, but the text of the adulatory song captures the rhythms of the *Hoshanna* hymns that we still recite. (The *Hoshanna* poems are among the oldest and most moving examples of Hebrew liturgical poetry, and inspired the efforts of many of our foremost synagogal poets.) The story also contains several clever "midrashic" expansions on the verses of the Hallel that would have been sung by Jews on the festival, then as today.

Anyone unfamiliar with the living practices of Jewish congregations would necessarily miss the point of the passage.

What Happens in the Hoshana Rabbah Moonlight?

The seventh day of Sukkot, which we refer to as "Hoshana Rabbah," was originally associated with the seasonal prayers for abundant precipitation in the approaching rainy season. The critical importance of rain for the Israeli ecology, combined with the powerful themes of divine judgment still reverberating from the previous weeks' holidays, have lent to Hoshana Rabbah many of the features of Yom Kippur itself. Thus it is often depicted as the occasion when the year's verdicts are finally and irrevocably sealed.

This idea is underscored in some of the day's synagogue practices: for example, the cantor wears a white *kittel* and chants some of the day's prayers to the melodies associated with the "Days of Awe."

The metaphysical stature of Hoshana Rabbah was progressively enhanced over the centuries, so much so that its original agricultural roots were virtually obliterated in the popular consciousness. This pattern was particularly pronounced in the Jewish mystical tradition, the Kabbalah, and has had far-reaching effects on Jewish folk beliefs and practices.

The foremost classic of Jewish mysticism, the *Zohar*, describes how on Hoshana Rabbah, the verdicts that were decreed on Yom Kippur are officially distributed to all mortals.

An eerie variation on this motif is encountered in the influential thirteenth-century biblical commentary of Rabbi Moses ben Nahman (Nahmanides). In his explanation of a peculiar Hebrew expression that is employed in the Torah to describe the defenselessness of Israel's enemies—"their protection [literally: their *shade*] is removed from them" (Numbers 9:14)—the "Ramban" suggested that "Scripture might be alluding to the well know fact that on the night of the 'sealing' [of the divine decree] the head of a person who is fated to die during the approaching year will project no shadow in the moonlight."

A later Jewish biblical exegete, Rabbi Bahya ben Asher, ascribed a figurative meaning to Nahmanides' tradition: A shadow symbolically marks out the place that a being occupies on the earth, and accordingly its removal demonstrates that that being no longer occupies a fixed or designated place in the sublunar world.

Many subsequent writers speak of this tradition, namely that in the moonlight of Hoshana Rabbah no visible shadow will be cast by the heads of individuals who are destined not to live out the year.

As we frequently find when investigating superstitions of this sort, it turns out that the medieval Jews were echoing beliefs that were widely held among their non-Jewish neighbors in northern and eastern Europe. However, the Christians, of course, associated the phenomenon with their own holidays.

One Jewish scribe gratefully recorded in a manuscript colophon that "on the night of Hoshana Rabbah of [1556] I observed the shadow of my head in the moonlight. Praised be God, for now I am assured that I shall not die this year."

Rabbi David Abudraham of Seville, in his fourteenth-century commentary to the Jewish prayerbook, tells disapprovingly of some people who were accustomed on Hoshana

Rabbah to venture outside, draped only in a sheet, which they removed after having chosen a spot where the outline of their shadow would be clearly distinguishable in the moonlight. These individuals would check not only for the dreaded missing head, but also for fingers and limbs whose absent shadows would surely foretell the imminent demise of close relatives and loved ones.

Rabbi Moses Isserles, the sixteenth-century Polish rabbi whose glosses on the *Shulhan Arukh* are a central pillar of Ashkenazic religious law, recorded that several prominent halakhic authorities discouraged this practice on the grounds that it appeared to invite misfortune. And in any case "most people are not sufficiently expert in these matters." He counselled that people ought generally to avoid delving into the future.

A more recent halakhic authority, Rabbi Barukh Epstein, summarized the theological issue succinctly: "God forbid that Jews should indulge in such speculations, when an instant's repentance has the power to overturn any unfavorable decree. We would do much better to place our trust directly in our Heavenly Father."

How Rowdy Can It Get on Simhat Torah?

For a day whose chief purpose is to celebrate the Jewish people's commitment to the Torah, Simhat Torah has an uncanny propensity for running afoul of conventional Jewish law. Many of the day's fundamental synagogue rituals—such as the calling of an unlimited number of individuals to the reading of the Torah and the participation of minor children in the service—are exceptions to accepted liturgical procedures.

This situation is indicative of the deep impression that popular custom has stamped on Simhat Torah. Indeed the entire institution of Simhat Torah owes its existence to custom: It was unknown to either the Bible or Talmud, and its earliest mentions are in the writings of the medieval Babylonian *Ge'onim*.

Furthermore, Simhat Torah is a day whose very essence is "rejoicing." Joy, especially when it is for such a sublime purpose, is difficult to rein in, and it is understandable that the participants have not always been scrupulous in giving consideration to the finer requirements of religious law.

The complex history of Simhat Torah has been punctuated by recurring skirmishes between popular enthusiasm and the rigors of the halakhah. The rabbinic leadership often found itself divided over the relative importance of adherence to legal standards and the encouragement of religiously motivated fervor.

In most cases the rabbis chose not to oppose the popular practices, pointing to the wholesomeness of the motives and the tenuous halakhic status of Simhat Torah as a mere "extra" day appended to Shemini 'Atzeret. On these grounds the rabbis overcame their initial objections to activities like dancing, hand-clapping—and sometimes even to the use of instrumental music—that should normally have been prohibited on festivals by talmudic decree. Later generations, under the influence of Kabbalah and Hasidism, would turn dancing into an inseparable part of the holiday celebrations.

This attitude of permissiveness was the characteristic response of the rabbinic leadership to the halakhic liberties that were taken in the festive merriment. Reluctant to alienate the common people, the sages went out of their way to invent contrived justifications for questionable practices.

Notable exceptions were the rabbis of eighteenth- and nineteenth-century Poland and Lithuania. Jewish society there had become polarized, and many rabbis regarded themselves as a learned élite that should keep at a safe distance from the vulgar masses. Several rabbis of the era expressed their open disdain for the notion that unlettered working folk, who did not occupy themselves in full-time religious study, could be included in a festival devoted to learning.

Now I don't know why it is, but common people have an irrepressible predilection for burning things as part of their celebrations, giving rise to potential violations of the biblical prohibitions against kindling and extinguishing fire on a festival. These customs became a recurrent concern of rabbinic responsa about Simhat Torah. For example, the Babylonian *Ge'onim* were questioned about the widespread practice of lighting incense in front of the Torah scrolls on the holiday. Children in fifteen-century Germany would ceremoniously burn the foliage that had hitherto adorned the tops of their newly obsolete sukkahs, a halakhically questionable procedure that was defended by no less an authority than the famed Rabbi Jacob Möllin, the "Maharil." In Worms it was customary for the rabbi to join in dancing around an immense bonfire that had been built for that purpose. In several communities, including Izmir, Aleppo, and Jerusalem, those individuals who were honored with special *'aliyyot* to the Torah were escorted from their homes to the synagogue in a spirited procession illuminated by candles and torchlight.

The rabbinic authorities in Izmir were divided about whether they should condone this last-mentioned practice. Some were ready to invoke a ban of excommunication against it. However, those who permitted the activity could point to its long history: Some of the most distinguished sages of previous generations had not seen fit to protest—indeed several of them had themselves marched proudly in the parades!

A Turkish rabbi who was reluctantly enmeshed in the controversy wrote with notable irony: "A flame ignited spontaneously during the lifetimes of those earlier rabbis, and the blazes will continue to burn with even greater fury among the leaders of the Izmir community, who have been split into two contending camps. . . ."

As if matters were not yet sufficiently volatile, several Jewish communities in central Europe and the Balkans developed an affection for detonating firecrackers and fireworks in the synagogue in honour of Simhat Torah. For some distinguished authorities, like the Polish Rabbi Abraham Gombiner, this constituted irrefutable proof of what happens when you let boorish commoners celebrate a scholars' holiday. However, even this practice found advocates among the respectable rabbinic leadership.

Thus, when asked to rule on the use of fireworks in the synagogue of Sarajevo (a fashion that had lately been introduced from Venice), Rabbi David Pardo reminded the opponents that the rowdy activities were inspired "by the joy of a commandment, and were for the glory of the Lord's perfect Torah, which has always sustained us and our forefathers, and which can be counted on to be forgiving. . . . "

Particularly outspoken among the defenders of firecrackers was Rabbi Elia Shapira, the distinguished head of the Prague yeshiva. His fierce diatribe aptly illuminates some of the social and psychological issues that underlay the controversy: "It is evident that the masses should be encouraged to rejoice as much as possible when it is to honor a mitzvah—contrary to the approach of those nay-sayers who would have us transform the joy into gloom, God forbid! Those people deserve to be censured for causing people to refrain from the joy of the commandments."

HANUKKAH

How Did the Maccabees
Become Christian Martyrs?

The frustration of constantly having to explain to non-Jewish neighbors that Hanukkah is not "the Jewish Christmas" serves to confirm the conviction that the Festival of Lights, as a supreme celebration of Jewish nationalism is, more than any other of our holidays, uniquely Jewish. Since it is not mentioned in the Bible, it does not make up part of the "common heritage" that we are supposed to share with Christianity.

In actuality this hypothesis turns out to be completely wrong. Seen from a historical perspective, the above thesis can be totally reversed: The principal documents of the events, which are contained in the first two "Books of Maccabees," were actually preserved not by Jews, but by the Christian Church. Our own talmudic sources retained only the vaguest of memories of the wars, preferring to emphasize other aspects of the festival, such as the laws of the kindling of the lamps and such peripheral tales as the miracle of the oil jar.

Among the Christians, on the contrary, the Books of Maccabees were, until very recently, accepted as part of their bibles. This was true of most of the older Protestant versions, including the standard King James English translation of 1611, and it is still the case in most Roman Catholic editions.

In order to understand how this came about we must transport ourselves back to Alexandria, Egypt, the home of one of the most renowned Jewish communities of antiquity.

GREEK AND HEBREW BIBLES

Like many of us today, most of the Greek-speaking Alexandrian Jews were not comfortable enough in Hebrew to read their Bible in the original and had to make use of a Greek translation. Their translation, which we loosely refer to as the Septuagint, after the Greek version of the Torah that was its earliest and most revered component, came to include Greek versions of the rest of the Hebrew Bible. The versions current in Alexandria also came to contain a number of other, later works (and expansions to biblical books). Among these latter works were included the Books of Maccabees.

With the development of the Christian Church, its leaders were quick to choose the Alexandrian Jewish Bible as its official Greek version. This choice reflected the veneration with which the Septuagint had long been regarded by the Jews, and also served special Christian interests: some central Christian claims for support from "Old Testament" prophecy made sense only in the Septuagint translation (for example, the doctrine of virgin birth originated in a mistaken rendering of Isaiah 7:14).

It is widely believed that it was because of the Septuagint's identification with the Church, and because it did not reflect the sophisticated exegetical (midrashic) methods being developed in Eretz Israel, that it came to be abandoned by the Jews, though the Talmud preserves the legend of the miraculous circumstances surrounding its composition.

Those works that were included in the Greek, but not in the Hebrew Bible, came to be known as the "hidden" books—the Apocrypha. Among these were the Books of Maccabees.

THE MACCABEE INSPIRATION

As a result of this development the persecutions of Antiochos Epiphanes, the heroism of the Jewish martyrs, and the military exploits of the Maccabees were all familiar topics to any medieval Christian who read his Bible. By contrast, Jews knew of the events only from incomplete translations into Hebrew that had been made from the Christian Apocrypha collections.

This is especially ironic when we recall how conspicuously Jewish the Books of Maccabees are in their religious attitudes and ideologies. At first Maccabees was composed in Hebrew, but the original has been lost, probably irretrievably.

As part of the Christian heritage, the events and personalities of the Hanukkah story were used as archetypes for distinctly Christian ideals and concerns. The ancient Jewish martyrs, ready to die for their faith, served as models of inspiration for Christians facing persecution at the hands of the Romans, even as Antiochos was perceived as a prototype of anti-Christian tyrants like Nero or Diocletian.

Like the Jews, the Catholics were generally more impressed with the accounts of martyrdom than with the military victories.

The only event from the Books of Maccabees to find its way into the Talmud is, I believe, the touching tale of the mother and her seven sons who stalwartly chose death rather than participate in idolatrous worship. This story is given special emphasis by Church tradition as well, and it is these martyrs, rather than the military heroes of the revolt, who are normally referred to as "the Holy Maccabees," and whose deeds are celebrated throughout the Catholic Church on August 1st—the only Old Testament figures to merit such an honor.

Imagine celebrating Hanukkah in the middle of summer!

At a later period, the religious militancy of the Maccabees was cited as a precedent for various holy wars, including the Crusades (whose victims were often innocent Jews) and other military campaigns initiated in the name of the faith.

The Maccabees' readiness to oppose the "legal" rulers of Judea inspired various Christian dissident groups who found themselves in rebellion against the State or against the official Church—an imagery that was drawn upon repeatedly during the Protestant Reformation (though the Catholics also found ways to see themselves as the legitimate heirs to the Maccabees).

Interestingly, the rise of autonomous nation-states in the modern era led to a re-interpretation of the Maccabean uprising. Those writers who proclaimed the supremacy of the State tended to favor the position of Antiochos. Thus, Voltaire (who was at any rate a virulent anti-Semite) praised Antiochos as the legitimate and cultured king of Judea, who justly tried to stamp out the disobedience of the barbarous Jewish rebels. This re-reading of events became even more popular among scholars with the rise of political anti-Semitism in Europe.

Perhaps the most welcome consequence of the familiarity of Christians with the story of the Maccabees is the way that it has also served as a source of inspiration to artists and composers. In particular, one feels a certain gratitude for the fact that G. F. Handel composed his oratorio "Judas Maccabeus," whose pompous themes fill the Israeli radio waves during the Hanukkah season, and serves as the only real alternative to the ubiquitous *Ma'oz Tzur* tune.

What Is the Spiritual Aura of Hanukkah?

Students of Jewish tradition have often noted the peculiar character of the religious celebration of Hanukkah. Whereas the history books tell us that the festival honors the heroism and ultimate victory of the Jewish rebels against their Hellenistic persecutor, the talmudic tradition focuses on one legendary event, the miracle of the oil, as the central moment of the story.

Of course, Hanukkah is not the only holiday in the Jewish year that commemorates national liberation. Both Passover and Purim celebrate our deliverance from national threats. And yet the characteristic observance of Hanukkah—the kindling of lights—is unique. This is a fact that has been discussed by traditional commentators.

On the surface Purim and Hanukkah commemorate similar events, yet Purim is a day of feasting and rejoicing, while Hanukkah confines itself to the more ethereal ritual of candle-lighting. Why the difference?

This is a puzzle that was discussed by one of the great talmudists of sixteenth to seventeenth-century Poland, Rabbi Joel Sirkes, usually known as the "BaH" (the acronym of his important legal commentary the *"Bayit Hadash"*). In this commentary Rabbi Sirkes proposes the following essential differentiation between the two ways of celebrating libera-

71

tion. The difference, he explains, cuts to the essence of each day's meaning. Purim, like Passover, recalls a threat to the physical survival of the Jews. Haman's plot was aimed against the Jews as a nation. He did not challenge them to abandon their faith or observances, but simply wished to get rid of them.

The persecutions of Antiochos, on the other hand, were of a different type. He did not want to kill Jews, but was concerned "merely" to pry them away from their religion. It was a campaign against the Jewish *spirit*, probably the first such threat in our history, and hence it is appropriate that it should be celebrated through lights, the least material of physical phenomena.

The Jewish commentators have drawn upon a rich set of associations in their efforts to explain the significance of the Hanukkah lights. Talmudic law emphasizes that light has the power to effectively spread the message afar, proclaiming the greatness of the Hanukkah miracle.

Several later commentators have compared the flames of the candles with the human soul itself, citing the words of Proverbs 20:27, "The spirit of man is the lamp of the Lord." For others, the lights are the lights of the Torah, in accordance with Proverbs 6:23: "For the commandment is a lamp and the Torah is light."

Maimonides, on the other hand, compares the Hanukkah lights to the Sabbath candles, whose purpose is to radiate an atmosphere of peace. "Great is peace," he concludes his discussion of the laws of Hanukkah, "for the entire Torah was given only to create peace in the world."

In the mystical tradition, the Hanukkah candles partake of a metaphysical aura. They are nothing less than the primordial light fashioned by God on the first day of the Creation. According to rabbinic legend this light, which preceded the creation of the sun and stars, was a spiritual illumination that allowed the first man to see to the ends of the earth.

The hasidic master Rabbi Pinhas of Koretz noted that this primordial light illuminated the world for thirty-six hours, until Adam's disobedience persuaded God to hide it away. Accordingly we kindle a total of thirty-six candles during the eight days of Hanukkah.

The midrash relates that after Adam's fall God put the original light in storage, not to be removed until the messianic era. It is through the same light of the Hanukkah candles, says Rabbi Pinhas, that the Messiah will one day redeem us, echoing the words of the Psalmist (132:17): "There have I ordered a lamp for my anointed one."

What Is Hellenism?

The villains of the Hanukkah story are identified as "Hellenizers." As with many villains of history, our sources are not very interested in the details of their ideology, beyond the fact that they came into a fateful conflict with our ancestors.

The phenomenon of Hellenism nevertheless presents certain difficulties that are deserving of our attention. For example, many of us are puzzled by the fact that the same Hasmoneans who led the struggle against Antiochos and his collaborators so quickly established a state that was itself modeled along Hellenistic lines. The same holds true to some degree for the literature of the Talmud and Midrash, which is filled with thousands of Greek words and reflects intimate familiarity with Greek society and customs. Both the Hasmonean kings and the talmudic rabbis were likely to bear Greek names. If Hellenism was the enemy, then how could loyal Jews have been so tainted by it?

The truth is that Hellenism is a much more complex phenomenon than is allowed for by the schoolbook accounts of the Hanukkah story. As understood by historians the term does not refer to the actual culture of ancient Greece, but to a synthesis between Greek civilization and that of the ancient Middle East.

When Alexander the Great's armies overtook these regions, Greek colonies were set up in order to spread the benefits of civilization to backward Semitic peoples. In practice, this would usually take the form of communities of Greek merchants or soldiers trying to maintain an Athenian lifestyle on Egyptian or Judean soil. The process was not one-directional however. Over a few generations, the original Greek settlers (who were not usually scholars or philosophers) would become assimilated and intermarried into their surroundings, soaking up many of the features of the local culture. It is this mixture of Greek and Middle-Eastern elements that is designated in the word *Hellenism*.

Last summer, a participant in a computer network devoted to the study of ancient Judaism requested from his colleagues that they share their characterizations of Hellenism. Several of the responding scholars offered the same analogy: the status of English-language culture in contemporary Israel. Thus, most Israelis are familiar with Coca-Cola™, television shows, and American consumer technology, but are far less likely to have read Shakespeare or Thoreau.

This description accurately parallels the situation in ancient times as regards Hellenistic culture. Talmudic literature uses an extensive Greek vocabulary for utensils and political institutions. There is, however, no evidence that the rabbis had read Plato or Sophocles. While Homer is apparently mentioned in the Mishnah (but only to forbid reading him), the only major philosopher to be mentioned is Epicurus, not so much as an individual but as a synonym for atheism or heresy.

This pattern held true for the Maccabean period as well. The Maccabees, like the rabbis, were "Hellenists," but they knew to draw the line when foreign ideas threatened sacred Jewish values and practices. It should be noted though that even the "real" Hellenists against whom the Maccabees were fighting were probably not trying to establish real Greek paganism in Jerusalem, but merely what they perceived to be a modified version of Judaism that would be more acceptable to Hellenistic conventions.

This less simplistic understanding of Judaism and Hellenism is of more than antiquarian interest. It may provide us with a more realistic criterion for applying the lessons of Hanukkah, and in making the complex choices between the mixed Jewish and "Hellenistic" options that actually confront us in our daily lives.

Why Is Hanukkah Considered a Women's Holiday?

There is little in the major themes of Hanukkah that would characterize it as a distinctively female holiday. Women do not figure prominently in either the military victories or in the miracle of the jar of oil. And yet Jewish tradition has emphasized that women have a special connection to the celebration, and in some communities they are accustomed to refraining from work while the candles are lit.

The basis for this tradition is in a saying in the Talmud by Rabbi Joshua ben Levi that "Women are obligated to light Hanukkah candles because they were included in the miracle." The commentators disagree over how precisely to understand this passage. Does it mean that women were merely counted as one segment of the whole Jewish people, all of whom were redeemed from Greek oppression? Or did they have some special role in the deliverance. The former possibility (which appears to be the view of the Jerusalem Talmud) finds support in the fact that a similar observation is made regarding Passover, in which story women did not have a conspicuous role. The latter possibility is suggested by the juxtaposition to Purim, in which Queen Esther was a key player.

Most traditional commentators have preferred to explain that women did indeed play a central role in the Maccabean victories. However, there is no consensus about what episode is being alluded to. A likely possibility would have been the heroic martyrdom of the mother and her seven sons, which was known to the author of the Book of Maccabees as well as to the Talmud. Yet few authors make reference to that episode, probably because it did not advance the miracle of the Jewish victory in any obvious way.

Rashi alludes cryptically to a different tradition, writing that "the Greeks had decreed that all brides would first be violated by the Greek officers, and the miracle was accomplished with the help of a woman."

The story to which Rashi is alluding is not attested in any of the standard talmudic or midrashic works. However, medieval manuscripts have preserved a number of similar tales that claim to reconstruct the origins of the Maccabean revolt. These accounts concur with Rashi that the Greek generals had claimed the "right of the first night" with Jewish brides (a motif that appears in other talmudic stories, without connection to Hanukkah), and add that one of the Hasmonean women—her precise name and family relationship vary in the different traditions—stirred her hitherto passive family into action by publicly stripping herself naked on her wedding day, shocking the people into avenging the sacrilege and humiliation of the daughters of Israel, even as Simeon and Levi had requited Dinah's honor.

Several medieval commentators supplement Rashi's words with additional details. R. Nissim of Gerona, citing a "midrash," states that the daughter of Johanan the Hasmonean fed cheese to an enemy general in order to make him drowsy, whereupon she proceeded to cut off his head, thereby allowing her companions to flee to safety. He notes that this was the origin of the custom of eating cheese on Hanukkah. Rashi's grandson Rabbi Samuel ben Meir (Rashbam) identifies the heroine of the story as Judith.

It is clear that these commentators were identifying Rashi's story with the ancient tale of Judith. According to the exciting story that has been preserved in the Greek Apocrypha, the lovely and virtuous widow Judith lived during the time of Nebuchadnezzar, and succeeded in saving Jerusalem from an invasion by the Assyrian general Holosfernes by pretending to seduce him, getting him drunk, and then decapitating him. The historical context is of course inappropriate to Hanukkah, and the detail about the cheese (which appears to have been copied from the similar exploit of Jael and Sisera in the Book of Judges) is absent from most versions of the Judith story. Although there is an interesting analogy when Judith invokes the precedent of Simeon and Levi's reprisal against Shechem, it is clear that we are dealing with a different event.

This fact did not impede the Jewish storytellers from grafting together the stories about the Hasmonean bride and the heroic widow, and including the resulting tale among the exploits of the Maccabean revolt. A fortunate consequence of this was a rekindling of Jewish interest in the Book of Judith, a charming and inspiring gem of our literature that might otherwise have been consigned to neglect.

Was Judah a "Hammerhead"?

Whathat would Hanukkah be without the heroism of Judah the Maccabee! His exploits in spearheading the military revolt against the Seleucid armies and their Jewish collaborators are meticulously detailed in the ancient books that bear that name: the Books of Maccabees, which have been preserved in Greek.

And yet, for all his importance for the subsequent destiny of Judaism, we do not really know the meaning of the name Maccabee that was attached to him. In fact, we are not even certain how to spell it correctly.

Unlike his father Mattathias, Judah is not mentioned by name in any ancient Hebrew sources like the Talmud or Midrash, nor even in the Hanukkah prayers. The earliest Hebrew documents that speak of him date from the Medieval period and were probably derived from Greek or Latin sources.

The "k" or hard "c" sounds of European languages can have two equivalents in Hebrew, the *kaf* or the *kof*. Therefore the original Hebrew epithet of "Judas Maccabeus" might have been spelled with either letter. The difference is of course a significant one in reconstructing the meaning of the name Maccabee.

Modern Hebrew has generally preferred the version with a *kaf*, a tradition that can be traced as far back as the tenth-century Hebrew compendium of Second Temple historical fact and legend known as the *Yosippon*.

This spelling furnishes support for an explanation that many of us were taught in school, that the name Maccabee is an acronym for the Biblical verse *Mi kamokha ba'elim Hashem*, "Who is like unto thee among the mighty, O Lord!" As generations of schoolteachers have told the story, Judah carried these inspiring words upon his standard as he marched off to battle.

As attractive as this story is, it can hardly be justified on historical grounds. It is not mentioned in any early sources, and Hebrew acronyms of that sort were not to come into common use until later generations.

Furthermore, it appears that the "cc" in the Greek version of the name "Maccabæus" is far more likely to represent a Hebrew *kof* than a *kaf*, since the latter is normally represented by the letter *chi*. If that is correct, then we must set out in search of a different etymology.

The most widely circulated explanation for this spelling connects the name to the Hebrew word *makkebet* or *makkaba*, which appears in the Bible and Talmud in the sense of "hammer." This of course conjures up the idea of the mighty warrior "hammering" and crushing his foes. This dramatic explanation is not an unreasonable one, though it too is no more than a hypothesis.

Some modern scholars, less concerned with drama and heroism than they are with historical precision, have proposed some variations on the hammer motif.

One theory that has always appealed to me calls our attention to a passage in the Mishnah that lists various blemishes and deformities that would disqualify a priest from serving in the Temple. One of the disqualified types is designated a *makban*, interpreted as one whose head is shaped like a mallet or hammer.

Thus, argues the proponent of this explanation, the great Judah the Maccabee was not being named for his fierceness on the battlefield, but rather he was being singled out for the peculiar shape of his skull.

If this should strike us as an unbecoming manner of referring to a national hero, we should recall that in earlier days, before the widespread adoption of family names, individuals with identical given names had to be told apart somehow, and a distinctive physical characteristic, even if unflattering, often served that purpose effectively.

This practice was especially common in ancient royal dynasties, where the same name could repeat itself over many generations. Thus, one of Judah's contemporaries was known as Ptolemy the Fat-Bellied, and a successor to the infamous Antiochos of the Hanukkah saga was referred to as "the Hook-Nosed."

Many innocuous-sounding family names that are now in common and unobjectionable use originated in physical epithets of just that sort. And when you think of it, does the name Judah the Hammerhead really sound any worse than Norman Schwartzkopf?

What Became of the Maccabees' Menorah?

W hen the victorious Maccabees returned to the des-
ecrated Temple they found that much of its wealth
and splendor had been plundered by the Greeks. Among the
artifacts that had been stolen by Antiochos was the golden
candelabrum, likely the same one that had been fashioned
by the returning Babylonian exiles in the time of Ezra and
Nehemiah. Until a new candelabrum could be crafted, the
soldiers improvised a makeshift device out of hollowed
spearheads. Only later was a new golden replica manufactured, which was probably lit at the official rededication of
the purified Temple, the first Hanukkah.

The last Hasmonean king, Mattathias Antigonos (40–
37 B.C.E.), chose to place an image of the menorah on the
coins minted under his regime. The symbolism was quite
appropriate: In addition to its associations with the Temple
(the coins proudly proclaimed Mattathias' position as High
Priest), the menorah served as a reminder of the heroic exploits that had brought his family to power as liberators of
their people.

The representation of the candelabrum on the Hasmonean coins provides us with our oldest picture of the
menorah. One notable feature of that depiction is that it
seems to be standing on a sort of tripod. This would agree

with the evidence of the Talmud (which speaks of an inde-
terminate number of "legs"), as well as with the three-legged
menorah images that were incorporated in much of Jewish
art in later centuries.

This portrayal of a menorah supported by a tripod base
is not the one that springs most naturally to our minds. Most
of us imagine the menorah with a broad, solid base, like the
one that appears in the official seal of the State of Israel. The
source for this image is the Arch of Titus, erected around
81 C.E. to commemorate the Roman triumph over the Jewish insurrection. On that arch we can see a meticulously
detailed relief of the spoils of Jerusalem Temple being carried through the streets of Rome, and the Menorah is perhaps the most prominent of the treasures. However the base
of Titus's menorah is not a tripod, but the now-familiar two-
tiered hexagonal structure.

There are many factors that testify to the authenticity of
the depiction in Titus's arch: In general, Roman triumphal
arches were designed as historical documents and toward that
end strove to be as accurate as possible. In this case, almost
all the details demonstrate the sculptors' intimate knowledge
of the Temple's vessels as described in the Bible and other
Jewish sources. Moreover, the proportions of the candelabrum, with its oversized base, are in such blatant conflict with
the classical notions of aesthetic form that it is inconceivable
that a Roman craftsman would have invented them.

How then are we to explain the discrepancy between
these two different renderings of the menorah's base?

Some clues to this mystery are suggested by the ornamental designs that appear in Titus's menorah. Though the
images have been eroded over time, it is possible to discern
vestiges of such figures as eagles and fish-tailed sea serpents
or dragons. A similar base has been excavated from a Roman
temple at Didymus, now in southern Turkey.

The eagles were, of course, the best-know symbol of Roman sovereignty. The dragons were a popular decorative motif in Roman art, and the whole candelabrum seems to testify to the strong Roman influence.

There are, however, some striking differences between Titus's candelabrum and its pagan counterparts. The Didymus lamp, for example, features a human figure, a water-nymph, seated on the back of the monster. It also portrays this creature with spiky rills issuing from its neck, an image that was explicitly prohibited by talmudic law. Both these features are lacking in the image of the Temple menorah. While both these facts argue for its Jewish origins, they cannot offset the strong Roman influence perceptible in the design.

As some scholars have observed, this mixture of a positive disposition toward things Roman, mitigated by a Jewish antipathy toward pagan images, fits the personality of King Herod, the despotic monarch whose prolonged and unpopular rule over Judea was made possible by his slavish obedience to his Roman masters. Throughout his career he tried to impose Roman social and religious institutions upon his reluctant subjects.

It is thus entirely characteristic of Herod's approach to introduce into the Temple itself a candelabrum that was adorned with the symbols of Roman authority and values. As in similar cases, Herod was unable to ignore completely the popular resistance to human images or explicitly pagan motifs.

If this is correct, then the Menorah that was plundered by the Roman legions was not the symbol of religious freedom that had been created by the Maccabees, but a despot's monument to foreign oppression.

This fact might account for the absence of the menorah from the coinage of the Jewish rebellions of 69 to 70 and

135, which made much use of other symbols from the Temple worship.

When the menorah did regain popularity as a decorative theme in Jewish art from the third century onwards, it was the original three-legged lamp that was chosen by the Jewish craftsmen as a symbol of religious pride and messianic hope.

What Is the Origin of *Hanukkah-Gelt?*

During the year that our family was sojourning in California, our children came home from school with marvelous reports of the gifts that their classmates had received in honor of Hanukkah: color televisions, Nintendos, and beyond. We had of course heard about the exaggerated commercialization of the American Hanukkah, but the phenomenon did not become tangible for us until that experience.

In comparison with the *mishloah manot* of Purim or the *afikoman*-bargaining of the Passover seder, gifts are not a traditional feature of Hanukkah observances.

The closest equivalent to an institution of gift-giving on Hanukkah is the Eastern European custom of distributing *Hanukkah-gelt* to the children. However, even this is of recent vintage, and it is hard to find mentions of it before the nineteenth century.

It would appear that *Hanukkah-gelt* evolved out of an earlier practice with a decidedly different character. Inspired by the semantic and etymological connections between *Hanukkah* (dedication) and *hinnukh* (education), some Jewish communities used the Hanukkah season as an opportunity to recognize their religious teachers and students. An interesting practical application of these ideals is related in *Hemdat Yamim*, a homiletical collection first published in eighteenth-century Smyrna, a work whose author's identity (other than the fact that he was a devotee of the messianic pretender Shabbetai Zvi) has continued to elude bibliographers.

The *Hemdat Yamim* reports that "in some communities, the custom has arisen of having the children distribute coins to their teachers along with other gifts. Other beggars make the rounds then, though the mitzvah is intended primarily for the benefit of impecunious students."

Rabbi Jacob Joseph of Polnoye, the renowned student of Rabbi Israel Ba'al Shem Tov, wrote that in Eastern Europe it was customary during Hanukkah for rabbis to make the rounds of outlying villages to strengthen Jewish education. Although initially the teachers were scrupulous about not accepting payment for their services, eventually they agreed to at least accept compensation for lost time. Before long the tour, with trademark lantern in hand, came to be seen by many as expressly intended for the collection of material tokens of appreciation, and this evolved into a quasi-obligatory gift of *Hanukkah-gelt*. *Hanukkah-gelt* tours are mentioned as a routine matter in some early hasidic stories, and the practice expanded to encompass additional recipients—such as preachers, cantors, butchers, and beadles—as well as a broader variety of acceptable currencies, including whiskey, grain, vegetables, and honey. The right to collect *Hanukkah-gelt* would be written into the contracts of communal employees, and legends were even circulated to the effect that one of the collectors might be none other than the prophet Elijah!

It is not until the nineteenth century that we begin to hear about *Hanukkah-gelt* being directed primarily at children. We are not certain how or why this transformation occurred, but it is described in several autobiographical memoirs, especially by children of well-to-do homes.

Variations on these customs were also observed in Sepharadic and Oriental communities. Poor Jewish children in Persia would go door to door offering, in return for gifts, to protect their benefactors' households from the Evil Eye by burning special grasses. In Yemen, it was customary for Jewish mothers to give their children a small coin on each day of Hanukkah, with which to purchase sugar powder and red coloring that would be used as ingredients for a special holiday treat: a sweet beverage known as "Hanukkah wine" that was drunk at their nightly parties.

In the "old yishuv" of Israel, Sepharadic yeshiva children circulated through the neighborhood asking for contributions of food for their festive Hanukkah feast. The little "Maccabees" in Hebron would reinforce their demands with toy rifles. In Jerusalem, the teachers made their own tour of the Jewish Quarter, serenading the householders with Ladino songs. The custom was believed to be linked to the week's Torah portion in which Jacob urges his sons to "go again and procure some food for us."

Needless to say, an immense gulf separates the customs described here from the shopping frenzy that is associated with the North American Hanukkah.

Where Is the Tomb of
the Last Hasmonean?

The Hasmonean dynasty, which leaped onto the stage of history with such dramatic heroism, disappeared from that same stage with cruel suddenness. The despot Herod, whose regime was forced upon the unwilling Jewish populace by his Roman overlords, was fully aware that the aura of Hasmonean charisma would constitute a continual threat to his power, and hence he undertook to murder ruthlessly all the remaining descendants of that family, including his beloved wife Mariamne, granddaughter of the Hasmonean ruler Hyrcanus II. Herod executed her on trumped-up charges of disloyalty, as he did afterwards to the two sons she had borne him, Alexander and Aristobulus.

The last Hasmonean actually to wield power was Antigonus, son of Aristobulus II, who succeeded, with the help of Parthian allies, in restoring Jewish autonomy for a few years (40–37 B.C.E.), until the young Herod persuaded the Roman rulers to send legions to uphold his own claim to the title of "King of Judea." Assisted by Roman and Edomite forces, Herod destroyed Antigonus' Galilean guerrillas in the caves where they were concealed. He then proceeded to besiege Jerusalem, where his forces conducted a wholesale carnage of the civilian population. Antigonus surrendered his person to the Roman general in the vain hope that the latter could be persuaded to treat his victims with greater compassion. In the end, Antigonus was led in chains to Antioch to be executed ignobly before Marc Antony.

A link to that tragic episode may have been revealed in 1971 when a bulldozer was preparing the foundation for a private house in Jerusalem's Givat Hamivtar district. As so often occurs in Israel, the excavation unexpectedly uncovered an archeological site, an ancient burial cave. As scholars and archeologists were summoned to examine the site, their attentions focused upon an extraordinary inscription facing the cave's entrance, composed in the Aramaic language in the "old Hebrew" alphabet in use among the Samaritans.

The inscription told a terse but moving story related in the first person by an individual who identified himself as "Abba descendant of Eleazar the son of Aaron the High Priest." This Abba goes on to describe how he was born in Jerusalem, but was subsequently "tortured and persecuted," and exiled to Babylonia. Now he has returned to his home bearing the remains of one Matathias son of Judah to bring them to final burial in this cave.

Many suggestions have been proposed to fill in the details of this tantalizing inscription. Although the old Hebrew script would seem to point to Samaritan origins, this would conflict with the importance assigned to Jerusalem as the protagonist's birthplace and the final resting place of the deceased. The Samaritans decisively rejected Jerusalem in favor of their own sanctuary on Mount Gerizim near Shechem.

Even more puzzling is the question of why an individual who takes such apparent pride in his priestly pedigree would subject himself to defilement through contact with a corpse, in defiance of the biblical laws of priestly holiness. Since the deceased was evidently not a close relation, the burial must have been perceived as an act of especial importance. Indeed talmudic religion attaches supreme importance to the *met mitzvah*, the obligation to arrange for the proper burial of a corpse for whom nobody else is caring. Could this have been such a case?

It did not take long for scholars to turn their attentions to the name of the deceased. The names Matathias and Judah are of course familiar from the Hanukkah story, and they reappear throughout the short history of the Hasmonean dynasty. We learn from their coinage that the Hasmonean rulers normally had both Hebrew and Greek names. "Antigonus" was always employed as the Greek equivalent for Matathias, and "Aristobulus" for Judah. The possibility thus emerged that the cave on Givat Hamivtar belong to none other than Antigonus, the last Hasmonean king!

While it remains within the realm of speculation, the theory provides plausible explanations for some of the riddles referred to above. We know that the Hasmoneans had a special affection for the old Hebrew alphabet, which appears prominently on the coins that they minted. The distinguished status of this king and national hero would warrant a priest's defiling himself to bring him to burial near the holy city. Since the Hasmoneans were a priestly family, it is possible that Abba was a distant relation or family retainer. It might even be significant that he traced himself directly back to Aaron, rather than to the rival (and pro-Roman) Zadokite line that constituted the priestly aristocracy during the Second Temple era, but to which the Hasmoneans did not belong.

Most intriguing is the description of the "tortured and persecuted" Abba whose forced exile from his homeland had likely resulted from activities against Herod and Rome. We may imagine that the Romans forbade proper burial to a rebel who had been executed in political disgrace, and that attempts to counter that prohibition had to be conducted at tremendous personal risk.

Though the jury is still out on the question of how to correctly interpret the evidence, the controversy should be seen as yet another example of the inseparable bond that binds our people to the personalities and exploits of previous generations.

Why Did the Menorah Offend the Magi?

In contemporary North America, Hanukkah is probably the Jewish holiday that has received the most widespread acceptance from the general public. It is acknowledged in the communications media and at the greeting-card counters, and menorahs are lit ceremoniously in public places.

This has not always been the case. Although in ancient decrees of religious persecutions (for example, under the Roman Emperor Hadrian or the Byzantine church) the celebration of Hanukkah or the kindling of its lamps was not usually singled out as a prohibited act, there have been times in our history when the observance of this holiday could entail grave dangers.

Such a situation is alluded to in the following question from the Babylonian Talmud: "Is it permissible to remove a Hanukkah lamp on account of the *Habbar*s on the Sabbath?" The assumption underlying the query is that the opposition of *Habbar*s to the Hanukkah lights was intense enough to constitute a serious threat to Jewish lives, thereby justifying a relaxation of the prohibitions against handling fire on the Sabbath.

Who were these *Habbar*s? The term is apparently taken from the biblical word designating a practitioner of charms and magic, but was applied by the Babylonian rabbis to the

Zoroastrian Mazdean priesthood—the "Magi"—whose religion dominated Babylonia throughout most of the talmudic era. The kindling and possession of fire raised touchy problems with respect to some central pillars of their faith.

The severity of the problem is evident from a story that is related elsewhere in the Talmud, in which a third-century rabbi was lying in his sick-bed in the company of some colleagues when a *Habbar* burst in and snatched away his bedside lamp, prompting the Jewish sage to quip: "Merciful God, it would be preferable to live under Thy shade, or even in the shade of the children of Esau (that is, the Romans)!" Though the lamp in this story was not a Hanukkah menorah, it was nevertheless considered an affront to the *Habbar*.

As the Talmud's commentators would explain, the problem had nothing to do with the religious character of Hanukkah, or with its themes of religious and national freedom. It was the *fire itself* that lay at the root of the antagonism.

The preservation of a sacred fire was a central feature of Iranian religion. It was a priestly duty to maintain the flames, usually in special fire-temples devoted to that purpose. There existed a hierarchy of different flames, and although lower flames (like the human spirit) could be upgraded by being brought to a higher flame, the opposite was strictly forbidden. The fires that burned in individual hearths were allowed only insofar as they were subordinated to the next-higher flame, and so on.

A medieval *Ga'on*, a successor to the Babylonian rabbis who still possessed traditions about the circumstances of earlier generations, wrote about how "during the reign of the Persians the *Habbar*s would make the rounds of all the Jewish households, where they would extinguish the lamps and gather the embers, which they would bring to their idolatrous fire-temple. They would not allow either the fires or the coals to burn through the night except for those which they kept in the temples." The Talmud elsewhere tells of the vials and bellows that would be used by the Mazdean priests in order convey the flames that had been profaned by infidels in order to refine them in the sacred flame at the temple of Varahran.

Another *Ga'on* linked the talmudic stories with a particular Zoroastrian festival observed in his own days, known as *Sadah* or *Sadag*. The origins and precise date of this holiday are not completely known, but it is described in the ancient sources as a winter fire-festival, designed to encourage the sun to prevail over the winter cold and darkness, which they perceived symbolically as the embodiment of Ahriman, the god of evil. The ceremonious kindling of fires was central to its observance, and we may readily appreciate how the Jews' public kindling of their own fires at that season could be seen as a profanation of their rites.

The historical context for these events is well-known to scholars. Until the beginning of the third century the Jews of Babylonia lived under the tolerant rule of the Parthians who were scrupulous not to interfere with the religious and legal autonomy of the various ethnic groups who inhabited their empire. That situation came to an end with the rise to power of the Persian Sassanian dynasty whose emperors saw it as their sacred duty to promote the ancient faith of Zoroaster. Although the Jews were usually able to maintain good relations with the ruling powers, there were times when the missionary zeal of the Persian priesthood constituted a serious threat.

The most formidable champion of militant Mazdaism was Kartir, who strove to make his faith the only legal religion throughout the Persian empire. Toward that end he gave high priority to the establishment of many new fire-temples. Although initially his fanaticism was held in check by the kings, by the end of the third century he was given free reign and encouragement in his activities. In a monumental inscription that has been preserved, Kartir boasts of his effective persecution of the Jews and other religious communities. Under this kind of atmosphere the joyous lighting of a menorah could become an act fraught with peril.

Nevertheless, then as at other times, the Jews were somehow able to weather the crisis, and the Hanukkah flames eventually succeeded in outlasting the cultic flames of their opponents.

WINTER

What Is the Proper Date
to Pray for Rain?

Jews are well accustomed to the fact that our religious calendar marches to a completely different rhythm from the
one that is in common use in the surrounding society. There
is, however, a conspicuous exception to that pattern: The day
on which we begin to pray for rain in our daily prayers (in-
troducing the Hebrew formula *Ten tal umatar*) is defined in
the Siddur by a date in the "civil" calendar, the fourth (or
sometimes the fifth) of December.

The origins of this anomaly go back to ancient times,
when the rabbis of Babylonia decreed that rain should not
be requested prior to the sixtieth day after the Autumnal
Equinox. The significance of this date is not explained in the
Talmud, and some scholars have suggested that for the
Babylonian farmers rainfall was considered a nuisance
before the conclusion of the date-harvest. Whatever the
reason, it is clear that the equinox, as a phase in the cycle of
the sun, is most conveniently calculated by the civil calendar, which is a solar one.

In the course of the Middle Ages the Babylonian practice came to be accepted—though not without a struggle—
by all Jewish communities outside the Holy Land. Israel
itself follows a different, earlier date, defined according to
the Jewish calendar (the seventh of Heshvan).

Initially many Diaspora communities followed the Israeli custom, but eventually the powerful Babylonian rabbinate succeeded in asserting its authority as the supreme arbiter of religious practice.

Thus, as an eminent contemporary halakhist has observed, normative practice has rejected the more reasonable precedents of praying for rain either when it is beneficial for our own climate, or when it is required in the Holy Land—in favor of the unlikely option of linking it to the climate of Iraq (the current inhabitant of the land that was formerly called Babylonia).

But the peculiarity of the situation does not end there. The Autumnal Equinox actually occurs on the twenty-second of September, so that the sixtieth day following should come out on November 20, *not* December 4!

The discrepancy originates in the methods that we employ for calculating the solar year. The Talmud assumes that a year consists of precisely 364 and one-quarter days and halakhic practice bases its calculations on that premise.

The calculation is very close, but it is not fully accurate, since an astronomical year falls eleven minutes and fourteen seconds behind that estimate. The margin is admittedly a tiny one, but when stretched across the centuries of Jewish history the minutes begin to add up. Every 128 years the Jewish reckoning pulls a full day ahead of the astronomical equinox.

The Catholic Church, aware that its traditional Julian calendar (based on the same assumptions as the Talmud's) had lost touch with the facts of nature, corrected the situation through the introduction of the Gregorian calendar in 1582, which involved turning the clocks ahead eleven days to adjust for the discrepancy! The Gregorian calendar cleverly regulates the frequency of leap years in order to keep the equinoxes in astronomic proportion. It has now become the accepted standard for most of the world.

Because the Jewish world has never introduced an equivalent adjustment, the cumulative error over the centuries now amounts to fifteen full days.

And the gap will continue to widen. Even as *siddurim* published a century ago instruct the worshippers to begin reciting *Ten tal umatar* on December 3 or 4, so in the year 2100 will the dates shift to Dec. 5 or 6—gaining three days every four hundred years.

If left uncorrected this will lead to some bizarre consequences, as the season for reciting *Ten tal umatar* keeps shrinking. Eventually it will advance all the way to Passover, which marks the termination of the rainy season, and will not be recited at all. Although this is a mathematical inevitability, don't hold your breaths. It is not scheduled to happen yet for another 35,000 years.

As often happens, the halakhic world tends to prefer its own traditional rules and definitions over ones that issue from the outside world. Some rabbis have taken note of the problem, but are reluctant to tamper with traditions. Almost none have discerned any cause for alarm.

After all, they argue, we live in faith that the Messiah will appear at any moment. Surely he will arrive before matters get out of hand, so why don't we just wait and let him deal with the problem!

FIFTEENTH OF SHEVAT

Who Is the Incredible Plant-Man?

"For the Tree of the Field is man . . ."

There exists a long-standing disagreement among the Jewish commentators about how precisely to read the words of Deuteronomy 20:19—as an assertion that "the tree of the field is essential to human life" or as a rhetorical question: "Is the tree of the field a man?!" Whichever reading we prefer, it seems clear that the Torah did not intend literally to equate human beings with trees or any other plants. Jewish literature does however contain references to a creature who is half-man and half-plant.

The Mishnah tractate *Kila'im*, which elaborates upon the biblical prohibitions against crossbreeding and hybridization, deals in meticulous detail with the botanical and zoological classifications of several species. In the course of its discussions it makes mention of a creature of doubtful classification, which it calls *adnei hasadeh* (probably to be translated as "men of the field"). The question discussed in that passage is whether such a creature is to be regarded as human or animal, or as a bit of both.

Commentators, traditional and modern, have been puzzled about what sort of creature this could be. The less imaginative authorities posit that the Mishnah is referring to some sort of ape or gorilla. The context seems to imply something more along the lines of a "missing link," maybe a talmudic incarnation of Bigfoot.

The Palestinian Talmud offers the following enigmatic explanation of the term *adnei hasadeh*: 'It is the "Man of the Mountain," and it lives from its navel. If it is cut at the navel it dies.'

The standard commentators understand that the Talmud was referring to a sort of plant-man who was joined to the earth by his umbilical cord. Such beliefs were widely held in ancient and medieval times.

The medieval French commentator Rabbi Samson of Sens (twelfth–thirteenth centuries) relates the following tradition:

> I have heard in the name of Rabbi Meir ben Kalonymus of Speyer that it is an animal known as the *Yadua*. Its bones are used in magic and it has a kind of large rope that extends from a root fastened in the earth. From this it grows like a cucumber or a pumpkin, except that its face, body, arms, and legs have human form. It is attached from its navel to a cord that emerges from the root, and no creature can approach within the radius of that cord lest the creature attack them. It constantly looks around and observes anyone who attempts to come within range of the cord to hunt it, so that no one may come near it. Instead, they must lure it away from the cord until it snaps, at which point it immediately dies.

This explanation was circulated in many subsequent commentaries though not all authorities were pleased with it. For one thing, the Mishnah seemed to be referring quite explicitly to an animal-man, not a plant-man. Maimonides for example, basing himself on popular books about the "wonders of the world" (the medieval equivalent of National Geographic television specials), suggests that the *adnei hasadeh* were human-like creatures that were known to emit human-like but indecipherable sounds.

The belief in the existence of animals that grow from plants was widespread in earlier generations. Medieval rabbinic literature knows of a persistent dispute among rabbinic authorities over the kosher status of a "bird that grows on trees." In accordance with the prevailing view of the time, a certain species of fowl (the "barnacle goose") was believed to grow either from barnacle shells attached to wood planks, or like a fruit attached (at the beak) from the branches of trees. Leading rabbis held differing views as to whether such creatures were to be treated as meat, fruit, or shellfish. Church authorities at the time were debating with equal vehemence whether the creatures were permitted during Lent. The *Shulhan Arukh*, by the way, rules that they are a species of fruit, and do not require *shehitah*.

A fascinating discussion of the *adnei hasadeh* question is contained in the commentary *Tiferet Israel* by the nineteenth-century scholar Rabbi Israel Lifschutz that is printed in standard editions of the Mishnah. Rabbi Lifschutz cites the plant-man tradition of Rabbi Samson of Sens but is reluctant to accept it. The problem is *not*, he emphasizes, because such a being is unknown to naturalists, "for there are found beneath the earth the bones of many creatures that are now extinct, such as the mammoth and others, which may have been killed off because they were too dangerous." Rabbi Lifschutz refers in several places in his commentary to the latest discoveries of paleontology and archaeology and argues that such revelations confirm the midrashic tradition that speaks of God creating and destroying many worlds before finally settling on our own.

Lifschutz's rejection of the plant-man tradition stems from another difficulty: Such a being, he argues, would violate the economic logic of nature. God does not endow his creatures with superfluous limbs or organs. If the plant-man draws all its nourishment from the soil, then it should not be born with mouth, arms, or legs. In any case, says the *Tiferet Israel*, the passage in the Palestinian Talmud that is understood to refer to a plant-man need not necessarily be construed that way.

Rabbi Lifschutz presents his own alternative identification: The reference, he says, is to the orangutan. In size and shape, the orangutan bears a strong resemblance to a human, and can be trained to hew wood and draw water, to wear clothing, and to sit at a table and eat with cutlery. (One gets the impression that the rabbi may have seen some performing in a circus.) And though in our time, he continues, they are found only in the jungles of central Africa, it is entirely conceivable that in talmudic times they also inhabited the cedar forests of Lebanon and Israel.

As in other places in his commentary, the *Tiferet Israel* presents a dazzling combination of traditional Jewish scholarship and lively fascination with the scientific wonders of the world around him.

By the way, Rashi, the foremost Jewish commentator, makes a brief allusion to the *adnei hasadeh* in his commentary to Job (5:23), where the phrase *"avnei hasadeh"* ("stones of the field") appears. Rashi claims that the expression is identical to the Mishnah's *"adnei hasadeh"* and refers to a "kind of human," as distinct from actual beasts of the field mentioned separately in the verse.

Louis Ginzberg, the distinguished twentieth-century authority on rabbinic literature, understood that Rashi was referring to werewolves. Belief in werewolves, vampires, and other assorted monsters was common among the Jews of medieval Germany (as it was among their Christian neighbors) and several case studies may be culled from works such as the twelfth-century *Sefer Hasidim* (the Book of the Pious).

PURIM

How Did Purim Turn into a Carnival?

L ike all the festivals of the Jewish calendar, Purim as we know it today is the product of a long history of development.

Ostensibly a commemoration of national deliverance from danger, we should have expected solemn ceremonies of thanksgiving such as characterize Passover and Hanukkah. The victory over Haman is, however, distinguished by a unique mood of high-spirited frivolity, colored by high alcoholic content and a general tendency to make light of matters that would be treated more reverently at other seasons.

ORIGINAL SOLEMNITY

The earliest descriptions of Purim celebrations, from the Second Temple and mishnaic eras, offer no indication of the irreverence that we associate with the festival. The emphasis is on the formal reading of the Scroll of Esther, which was to be conducted with great care and seriousness.

To the best of my knowledge none of the familiar themes of drinking, parody, and so forth, are mentioned in talmudic sources emanating from the Land of Israel. In fact, the chief

Palestinian rabbinic exposition of Esther, the midrash *Esther Rabbah*, seems to take every possible opportunity to emphasize the dangers of wine, incorporating a lengthy tract on the virtues of temperance.

The events of the Megillah are interpreted as reflections of the religious behavior of the Jews of the time, and within the context of broader historical themes, especially the destruction of the First Temple and the beginnings of the building of the Second (which the rabbis believed was delayed by Ahashverosh and Vashti).

It was the Jews of Babylonia who seem to have introduced some of the more frivolous customs into the observance of Purim. Two main factors can be traced to the Babylonian Talmud: "Purim-Torah" and the encouragement of drunkenness.

IN THE BABYLONIAN TALMUD

An exceptional passage in the "Bavli" (Hullin 139b) serves as a model for subsequent "Purim-Torah"—that is, playfully using some of the far-fetched methods of talmudic logic and biblical exegesis in order to reach absurd conclusions.

The passage in question relates how a visiting rabbi was challenged to find references to Mordecai, Esther, Haman, and Moses (!) in the Pentateuch. The sage responds to the riddles with audacious, clever puns. For example, ignoring the traditional vocalization, he finds an allusion to Haman in Genesis 3:11: "Is it from (*hamin*) the tree . . ." (also hinting at the villain's hanging); and to Esther in Deuteronomy 31:18, where God says, "I will surely hide (*haster 'astir*) my face" (recalling Esther's refusal to disclose her origins to the king).

Typically, some of the later commentators approached the talmudic passage without full appreciation of its humorous intent. Thus Rashi gravely tries to justify the need to find an "allusion" to Moses' name in the Torah.

Or to take another example, the later custom of donning masks and costumes on Purim—a practice that is first reported in Provence in the early fourteenth century, and later achieved popularity under the influence of the German *Fastnacht* celebration and the Italian carnivals—was afterwards tied to the idea of God's "hiding his face" as found in the Talmud!

In contrast to the approach taken by the Palestinian sources, the Babylonian Talmud records the famous dictum of the noted sage Rava (*Megillah* 7b): "A man is obligated to get drunk on Purim to the point where he can no longer distinguish between 'Cursed is Haman' and 'Blessed is Mordecai.'"

Here, too, later authorities had trouble accepting the ruling at face value. For an arch-rationalist like Maimonides it was unimaginable that the *halakhah* could be condoning such actions; hence he re-interpreted the ruling to refer to drinking only enough to fall asleep. Some authorities understood that the statement was rejected by the Talmud, a view that it indicates by juxtaposing to it an incident wherein Rabbah slaughters Rabbi Zera while under the influence. (Rabbah is able to revive his colleague, though the latter politely refuses an invitation to the next year's festivities.)

MEDIEVAL PARODIES

From these talmudic beginnings we can trace the development of a whole genre of Purim parodies, wherein Jews would affectionately poke fun at the world of Talmud and *halakhah*. From the twelfth century, Jews in Italy, southern France (Provence), and elsewhere were producing parodies on the Talmud, liturgy, and other familiar pillars of Jewish life.

A typical Purim Tractate (*Masekhet Purim*) might follow the form of the tractate *Pesahim*, which deals with the regulations of Passover, except that all the stringent laws concerning the removal of leaven are now applied to water and non-alcoholic beverages, which are not to be tolerated on the holiday.

A special roster of biblical and rabbinic authorities populates these works. Alongside such drunkards as Noah and Lot we might encounter the prophet Habakbuk ("the Bottle"); as well as Rabbi Shakhra ("Drunkard"), or the commentary of Rasha ("Wicked"). In modern times especially, the format has been used to satirize a variety of social phenomena, from American Judaism to Israeli politics.

It might be my imagination, but I have noted that in recent years it has become almost impossible to find these parodies, which used to be routinely reprinted before Purim. This might be indicative of an excessively defensive mood that has overtaken religious Jewry.

Particularly among German Jews there also developed the institution of the "Purim-shpiel," a rowdy play on the Megillah story (or other theme) traditionally performed on Purim. Absorbing a number of different traditions, from the German theater as well as from Jewish exegesis, these productions took great liberties with plot and characterization, such that Mordecai might appear as a pathetic buffoon, Haman as a tragic figure, and so on. Such irreverence could of course be tolerated only during Purim.

To German Jewry we also owe the adoption of the hamantasch, a variant of the German *mahn-tash* ("poppy-pocket") pastry, given a new meaning for the occasion.

Our custom of sounding noisemakers at the mention of Haman's name is also a version of an old practice, which took on different forms through the generations. The earliest sources (from the writings of the Babylonian *Ge'onim*) speak of burning effigies of Haman on a bonfire. In medieval Europe children would write Haman's name on stones or wood blocks, and bang them until the name was erased.

In our observance of Purim we are thus drawing from a long line of historical precedents and developments.

Why Was There a War against Purim?

The talmudic sages were well aware that in adopting the Book of Esther and the festival of Purim as parts of biblical tradition, they were opening a door to some potential problems in public relations.

In one remarkable passage, the rabbis created a fictitious dialogue between Esther and her contemporary sages that must reflect the sort of rabbinic debates that were taking place in the first century over the acceptance of the Scroll of Esther into the scriptural canon: When Queen Esther asked that her book be included in the Bible, the rabbis are said to have responded, "You will awaken animosity between us and the nations!"

Jews over the ages must have often felt discomfort at the vengeful mood that seems to characterize Jewish-Gentile relations in this book, and may have frequently looked over their collective shoulders to check who was listening to the recital of the Megillah.

HAMAN THE JEW

In the early Christian Church, there was also considerable reluctance about accepting Esther into their Bible. It was not until 397 C.E. that a formal decision was made to accept it, in the Greek version that included a number of additions of a more palatable religious nature, including prayers of Mordecai and Esther that are lacking in the Hebrew.

Esther was seen as a symbolic representation of the Church, and Haman (who died by crucifixion, according to rabbinic legend) as an antithesis to Jesus. In an extreme (but almost inevitable) example of such allegorical role-reversals Haman was made to represent the Jews, and Vashti, the synagogue!

Even so, not all Christians were at peace with the inclusion of Esther in holy scripture. Martin Luther, the leader of the Protestant Reformation and one of history's most outspoken anti-Semites, did not hesitate to complain, "I am so hostile . . . to Esther that I wish it did not exist at all; for it Judaizes too much and has heathen perverseness."

Unlike other works of the Hebrew Bible, whose national context could be universalized, Esther was too much a celebration of undiluted Jewish national feelings—a fact that Luther could not stomach.

ITALIAN CARNIVALS

In other countries of the Diaspora different sorts of objections were being raised against Purim.

In Italy, for example, the Catholic authorities were particularly disturbed by the carnivals that came to be associated with the holiday (a feature that had been popularized by the Italian Jews). The Jewish celebration fell during the somber Lenten season, and proved an attractive source of relief for Christians looking for amusement. Church authorities in sixteenth-century Venice came to fear that Judaism might appear too attractive, and tried unsuccessfully to enforce separation of the two communities during the festivities.

The founders of the Jewish Reform movement, who were much concerned with making Judaism respectable in the eyes of their Christian neighbors and with defining Judaism as a system of beliefs devoid of any parochial, national, or ethnic associations, were equally uncomfortable with the Book of Esther and the celebrations associated with Purim.

"Enlightened" German scholarship, not bound by the religious reverence that had moderated earlier Christian assessments of Esther, were quick to pounce on the Megillah as an example of blood-thirsty Jewish chauvinism.

MORAL CORRUPTION

As early as 1790 an article appeared in a Berlin Jewish monthly suggesting that Jews abandon the observance of Purim because it fomented moral corruption, since Jews were secretly equating the ancient Persians of the biblical story with their own Christian contemporaries.

A defense of Purim was written in response by David Friedlaender, a distinguished student of Moses Mendelssohn. Friedlaender argued that among Prussian Jews, at least—who were cultured and devoted to their fatherland—no such suspicions need be entertained. The festivities even encourage generosity and charitable activities.

However, in a manner typical of his disdain for the uncouth traditionalist Jewish masses, Friedlaender adds that the way the average Jew celebrated Purim, though not immoral (since the noise he makes on hearing Haman's name is merely a mechanically performed habit, done unthinkingly like all other Orthodox religious rituals), is surely disgraceful. Such a Jew spends the whole morning at synagogue in anticipation of the gluttonous feast that awaits him at home.

Friedlaender, by the way, was later to achieve notoriety when he offered to convert to Christianity, on the condition that he not be required to accept any distinctly Christian dogmas or rituals. In the end he did not go through with the conversion. The "universalistic" Protestant clergyman to whom he had submitted his offer insisted that it be accompanied by an acknowledgment that Christianity was a superior religion, an admission that even Friedlaender, embittered as he was with his Judaism and his Jewish community, was not prepared to concede.

Such attitudes were to typify the responses of the Reform leadership. Abraham Geiger, one of the giants of nineteenth-century Jewish scholarship and the principal ideologist of the movement, observed that the Book of Esther was marred by "bad taste and mean feelings."

A twentieth-century Reform thinker, Schalom ben Chorin, actually proposed, in 1938, the elimination of Purim and the removal of Esther from the Jewish Bible, arguing that "both festival and book are unworthy of a people which is disposed to bring about its national and moral regeneration under prodigious sacrifice."

In retrospect, we can look back with considerable sympathy at the misgivings expressed by Queen Esther's rabbinic advisers. Indeed, Purim does have a way of arousing animosities among our gentile neighbors, especially where the hostility is there in the first place.

Conversely, the degree to which Jews are willing to openly celebrate this story of national deliverance can serve as an accurate gauge of our feelings of security, Jewish pride, and positive self-image.

Was Vashti a
Feminist Heroine?

V ashti has become one of the favorite heroines of the Jewish feminist movement. This much-maligned queen, the argument goes, should be appreciated as a positive role model, a woman who dared to disregard a royal decree that would have her displayed as a sex object before King Ahashverosh's rowdy drinking companions. Her ultimate downfall should accordingly be viewed as a martyrdom to the cause of sexual equality.

The rabbis of the midrash were not so sympathetic to the fate of the queen. This attitude can partly be explained on the grounds of their belief in divine justice: God would not have allowed her to be punished unless she had in fact done something to deserve it. We cannot, however, deny that the sages shared a certain sympathy with the king's basic assumptions. At one point they ridicule him for having to assert publicly "that every man should bear rule in his own house" (Esther 1:22), since this is so patently obvious as to go without saying!

However, the rabbinic vilification of Vashti cannot be explained entirely as a manifestation of male chauvinism. We must keep in mind that the Jewish sages tended to view the heroes and villains of the Bible not as individuals, but as instances of recurrent historical patterns. Vashti, they learned, was in fact the great-granddaughter of the arch-villain Nebuchadnezzar, King of Babylon, who had destroyed the sacred Temple. Vashti's ruin embodied the final stages of her grandfather's defeat, as foretold by the prophet Isaiah (14:22): "And I will rise up against them, saith the Lord, and cut off from Babylon name and remnant, and offshoot and offspring." Vashti's downfall marked the final cutting-off of the Babylonian royal offspring, following a pattern of typological thinking that has been applied in recent days to the likes of Saddam Hussein.

It was of course not enough to have Vashti penalized for the sins of her ancestor. The rabbis tried to show that she was culpable on her own "merits." For one thing, they insisted that Vashti had actively continued to pursue her ancestor's policies, lobbying against any royal inclination to rebuild the Temple in Jerusalem.

In their determination to show how Vashti had deserved her fate, the Jewish sages followed the midrashic method of deducing her crimes from the nature of her punishment, assuming that God always metes out justice measure for measure.

A clue to her misbehavior was the fact that the king's summons to her had come "on the seventh day, when the king's heart was merry with wine" (Esther 1:10). Surely this did not refer to the seventh day of the feast, since Ahashverosh had presumably been merry with wine from the beginning. The allusion must therefore be to the seventh day of the week, the Jewish Sabbath. Vashti was ordered to appear naked before the King on a Sabbath as a fitting punishment for enslaving Jewish maidens and forcing them to work on their day of rest.

The question remained: If she was really such a depraved creature, then why would she have declined an opportunity for exhibitionism? Here as well, the rabbis had to add some supplementary details to the biblical narrative: Vashti was indeed willing to display her charms before the king's drinking partners, but God had interfered by inflicting upon her a humiliating physical deformity. According to one view Vashti succumbed to leprosy. According to another one, the angel Gabriel came "and fixed a tail on her."

This last possibility was widely understood as a euphemism for a miraculous transformation to male anatomy. This interpretation was too risqué for some readers, and the offending sentence had to be censored out of some editions of the Talmud. In Louis Ginzberg's compendium of midrashic lore *The Legends of the Jews*, the passage appears (in the footnotes), but in Latin.

In its own way the midrashic tradition tried to "liberate" Vashti, portraying her as a wily politician, not merely a passive royal ornament. As the scion of a once-mighty royal dynasty, she would flaunt her pedigree in Ahashverosh's face. She was also adept at subtle political maneuvering. For example, the fact that she held a separate feast for the ladies of the imperial nobility, rather than participating in the general festivities, was interpreted as a wise strategic move: In case a coup should be attempted during Ahashverosh's celebration, she would have under her control a prestigious group of hostages to use as a bargaining card. We see, by the way, that the use of "human shields" as practiced by Saddam Hussein is not a recent innovation in that region of the world.

Whether or not these details justify her inclusion among the pioneers of women's liberation, Vashti remains one of the most fascinating and enigmatic figures in the Purim story.

Was Esther the
First Marrano?

The book of Esther does not explain why Mordecai insisted that Esther conceal her Jewishness from Ahasuerus. The traditional commentaries suggest a variety of reasons for this tactic. After surveying several of these explanations, the twelfth-century commentator Rabbi Abraham Ibn Ezra offers his own theory:

"Mordecai acted in this way so as to allow Esther to observe the Torah in secret, and not have to partake of non-kosher food. This would also enable her to keep the Sabbath without the servants noticing. For if her Jewishness were to become known, then the king might compel her to violate her religious traditions or have her put to death."

As some scholars have observed, the vivid picture of Jews covertly practicing their religion, in constant fear of being unmasked by domestic servants, might very well reflect conditions during Ibn Ezra's lifetime. At around the middle of the twelfth century, Spain and North Africa came to be ruled by a dynasty of fanatical Muslim fundamentalists known as the "Mu'ahadin" who forced many Jews to convert to Islam. It was this development that forced Maimonides' family to flee from Spain to Egypt, and Maimonides himself devoted a special letter guiding and encouraging the Jews in the face of this crisis.

From Ibn Ezra's description of Esther's plight, we see that already under this early persecution, long before the rise of the Christian Inquisition, Spanish Jews had learned to evade the threat of forced conversion by publicly professing the legal religion, while doing their best to observe their Judaism in secrecy.

From the perspective of the *halakhah*, the phenomenon of "Marranism," or crypto-Judaism, is difficult to justify, yet it was especially prevalent among Jews in Islamic countries. Under equivalent circumstances, German and French Jews were more likely to submit to martyrdom for their faith.

Some historians have suggested that the roots of this attitude should be sought in the mind-set of Islam, which permitted religious dissembling in order to save the lives of oppressed Muslims. It is likely that the Jewish response to such situations was influenced by the religious attitudes that were prevalent in the Islamic environment.

Whatever our views on the above question, there is no denying that the figure of Esther, covertly practicing her Judaism in a hostile foreign world, bears a strong resemblance to the situation of the Spanish and Portuguese *conversos* of later generations. Therefore, it should not come as a surprise that the story of Esther became a favorite source of inspiration to those Jews in their time of peril.

Significantly, the Inquisitional guidelines single out the observance of the "Fast of Esther"—even more than that of Purim itself—as a well-known indication of "Judaizing" activity. Because the Hebrew lunar calendar was not accessible to most Jews, the date of the fast—like those of all Jewish holy days—was calculated according to dates in the Christian calendar, and was to be observed on the full moon of February.

Because the fast could be kept through inaction rather than through any identifiable rituals, it became one of the most widely observed Marrano holidays, a substitute for Purim itself, whose observances were too visible to be safe. Furthermore, after generations of living as Christians, the Jews often perceived their Judaism in terms of Christian concepts; and since fasting was a favorite practice among pious Catholics, the Jews applied it wherever possible to Jewish contexts.

The Megillah of the Marranos was significantly different from our Hebrew text. The possession of Jewish religious books was of course prohibited by the Inquisition, and the Marranos obtained most of their limited knowledge of their tradition and history from reading the Old Testament of the Christian bibles. The Catholic "Vulgate" text of the Bible derives from the ancient Greek versions that contained extensive additions to the Hebrew text. (Ironically, several of these additions also appear in the prohibited Jewish *midrashim*.)

One of these "Catholic additions" to the Megillah was a moving prayer that Esther uttered before approaching the presence of Ahasuerus. In her entreaty she beseeched the Lord to deliver the Jews from the hands of the blasphemous oppressor into whose power his people had been given as a punishment for their sins. Esther herself proclaimed her disdain for the life she had been living among the heathens, compelled to eat at their tables and drink the wine of their offerings.

This version of the Book of Esther, which expressed so poignantly the feelings of the crypto-Jews of Spain, became one of their most beloved texts, and it was reported that at least one Jewish woman who was condemned by the Inquisition in Mexico—women were prominent among the spiritual leaders and heroes of the Marranos—knew how to re-cite it both forward and backward!

Through such tragic associations Jewish history has pro-vided continual fulfillment of the Megillah's declaration that the days of Purim *"should be remembered and kept through-out every generation . . . and these days of Purim should not fail from among the Jews, nor the memorial of them perish from their seed."*

Is the Purim Story an Astrological Myth?

O f all the possible names that might have been selected for the holiday commemorating the Jews' deliverance from Haman's decree, Purim ("lots") has never struck me as the most obvious choice. It refers to a relatively incidental feature of the story, when Haman used a lottery in order to select the appropriate date on which to execute his plot. It is not immediately obvious why this particular detail was considered significant enough to lend its name to the entire festival.

The rabbis of the Midrash tried to reconstruct the process by which Haman went about choosing the suitable date. In one version he is depicted as consulting the astrological symbolism that attached to each month of the year, rejecting them one at a time because their Zodiac signs held favorable associations for the Jews. At length he was left with Adar, governed by Pisces. Against Haman's reading that this was an omen of Israel's being swallowed up like so many fish, the Almighty retorted that fish can be predators as well as prey.

In the eyes of many medievals, astrology was accepted as irrefutable science, and several Jewish commentators were proud to discern allusions to that discipline in the pages of the Hebrew scriptures. Probably the most notorious of this group was the twelfth-century exegete Rabbi Abraham Ibn Ezra, who never passed up an opportunity to reveal the astrological roots of biblical stories and laws. True to form, in his commentary to Esther he amplified the midrashic tradition about Haman's consideration of the Zodiacal associations. He observed that the preference for Adar as a time for massacring Jews lay in the fact that Capricorn was aligned with Aquarius, Israel's sign. Several other commentators underscored that the inauspicious character of the day was governed by the convergence of celestial forces.

In a similar vein, Rabbi Bahya ben Asher envisaged the Purim story as a cosmic battle between heavenly powers: The beneficent influences of Venus and Jupiter were embodied in the persons of Mordecai and Esther, which were arrayed against Ahasuerus and Haman, who served as agents of the malevolent Saturn and Mars. The peril that threatened the Jews was thus of cosmic proportions.

All this invites the objection: If the influences of the stars are truly decisive in determining the destinies of mortals, then how did it happen in the end that Haman's plot failed?

According to several authorities, this is precisely the key to correctly understanding the miracle of Purim, for a divine decree in defiance of a horoscope is as much a marvel as the suspension of any other law of nature. Most Jewish exegetes drew attention to the fact that divine interference was necessary to counteract the supernatural threat.

While some commentators were content to see the Almighty prevail against the forces of stellar destiny, others took the theme much farther, discerning in the Purim story an outright rejection of the efficacy of astrology. The fifteenth-century Spanish Rabbi Abraham Shalom believed that this was the main issue in the struggle between Mordecai and Haman. The latter, as the descendant of Israel's primordial foe, the Amalek, held a consistently mechanistic view of a universe governed by the unchangeable course of the stars. Mordecai's refusal to do obeisance to Haman followed from his commitment to the Jewish idea of a God who transcends nature, and who has bestowed upon humans the ability to make free moral choices.

Thus, although we might initially seem far removed from a "primitive" world in which supposedly intelligent people believe in horoscopes, there is nevertheless a decidedly contemporary ring to the medieval debate. If for "astrology" we were to substitute "physics" or "genetics," then we would find ourselves in the midst of a thoroughly modern argument about how far scientific method can be applied to matters of human values and spirituality.

Then as now, the question elicited a broad range of responses. At the extremes, there were fanatical rationalists (especially among the Jewish followers of the Arabic philosopher Ibn Rushd) who sought to provide scientific explanations for the miracle tales of the Bible; as well as pious fundamentalists who tried to isolate themselves entirely from the heresies of scientific progress.

It would appear however that most Jewish thinkers tried to steer a delicate middle course in which scientific integrity did not demand the abandonment of religious values. It was this ideal that was epitomized in their assertion that Haman's astrological prognostications stopped short of determining the destiny of the Jewish people.

NISAN

What Is Special about the Month of Nisan?

For most of us, the Hebrew month of Nisan derives its distinctiveness from its association with Passover. Although we now think of it as the seventh month, we should not forget that for most of our history Nisan was counted as the first month, and the foremost among the months.

Earlier generations regarded the first day of Nisan as a special occasion in its own right that was celebrated in a variety of ways. This was especially evident during the era of the Second Commonwealth, an age noted for the proliferation of different Jewish sects.

An intriguing example can be found among the Dead Sea Scrolls, in a document known to scholars as the "Temple Scroll." This manuscript consists of a lengthy paraphrase of the Torah, interspersed with many additions of laws peculiar to the sect that produced it. According to the fragmentary remains of this document the first day of Nisan was to be observed as a full-fledged festival with special sacrificial offerings similar to those of Rosh Hashanah.

Several of the books that were held sacred by the Dead Sea sect made a point of identifying events in the lives of the Hebrew patriarchs and other biblical figures as having occurred on the first of Nisan. One of these, the Apocryphal "Book of Jubilees," relates how Noah had celebrated that

137

date as a holiday precisely according to the sacrificial regulations that are set down in the Temple Scroll. The same date was said to mark other events in the lives of the Hebrew patriarchs.

None of these sources ascribe the importance of the first of Nisan to its associations with the Egyptian exodus. More relevant for them was the fact that the inauguration of the Tabernacle and the ordination of the first priests had commenced on this date.

Rabbinic Judaism treated the eight-day ordination ceremony that had been observed in Moses' time as a one-time affair. For the Dead Sea sect, however, this was a fixed holiday that was ordained to be celebrated every year through special sacrificial offerings.

Though (unlike the Qumran sectarians) the talmudic rabbis did not accord it full festival status, they did have another special reason for celebrating the first of Nisan: This was the day in which the Temple began to purchase offerings from the new annual fund of *shekels*. For the Pharisaic sages the way in which the Temple's needs were financed was more than a fiscal question. By insisting that each Jew throughout the world pay an equal share each year, and that no individuals be permitted to purchase public sacrifices out of their own pockets, they were actively asserting the equality of all Jews in worship, a position that aroused concerted opposition among the aristocratic priests of the Sadducee party.

According to the ancient work known as *Megillat Ta'anit* the first eight days of Nisan were designated as a time of rejoicing precisely because they commemorate the victory of the egalitarian Pharisaic position over the elitist view of the Sadducees. We still acknowledge this festive quality through the omission of the penitential *Tachanun* prayers during these days.

Such was the quality of Second Temple Judaism with its many competing interpretations of just about every aspect of Judaism. It makes one wonder: With all these reasons for celebrating, where did our ancestors find time for their Passover cleaning?

PASSOVER

Why Is the Seder Like a Roman Banquet?

F ew seasons of the Hebrew year are as filled with symbolic ceremonies as the seder, the complex order of the Passover evening meal. Many of these symbols are easily understandable expressions of the ideas of freedom, thanksgiving, and identification with the sufferings of our ancestors. Some, however, appear curious or anachronistic and demand further explanation.

It is the nature of a living tradition that it is constantly attaching new dimensions of meaning to older symbols. The same ceremony may express different ideas and values (or at least express these values in a different language) to different generations. Frequently, these explanations become so persuasive that we lose sight of the original aims of the rituals.

As an example, let us look at the manner of sitting at the seder. The *Haggadah* tells us that we must sit leaning toward the left, and this is one of the peculiarities that the children are supposed to wonder at in the *Mah Nishtanah*. As we prop the pillows up against the chair-backs and do our best to keep them from falling onto the floor, we explain to ourselves that this is the way in which "free men" are supposed to sit.

Further reflection prompts the question: Which free men are we really talking about? Is there a class of free men that is known for sitting down at a leftward tilt?

The Talmud explains that the reason for leaning leftward is a medical one: otherwise we would choke on our food. Nonetheless, one wonders why this would be less likely to happen if we were leaning, say, backward.

The truth, of course, is that the reclining that is mentioned in the talmudic writings does not refer to leaning on pillows in a straight-backed chair, but to lying on one's side on a couch eating from a private little table, as was the custom at Roman feasts (and as we often see in historical epic films). Such aristocratic feasts were taken by the talmudic rabbis as a model of independence and freedom, and if you are right-handed, lying in such a position, supporting yourself with one arm, it certainly is recommended that you lie on your left side so that the right arm will be free to manipulate the food.

Given that we no longer recline in the manner of the ancients, and that such reclining would not in any case typify free men in our society, is it necessary still to observe such symbolic leaning?

This issue was debated by the medieval rabbis, who took different views. Some insisted that the symbols of freedom should conform to the standards of the society in which one lives. If the aristocracy is accustomed to sitting normally at a feast, then it would be nonsensical for us to lean. Others argued that talmudic traditions are not to be lightly tampered with, and the more curious and unusual the practice is, the more it should be encouraged, in order to arouse the interest of the children through the evening.

The Roman or Greek feast served as a model for a number of additional practices that we encounter at the seder. Modern scholars have pointed to the remarkable similarities between the structure of the seder and that of the ancient Symposium (such as the one described by Plato in the dialogue that bears that name) in which people would assemble over a festive repast to discourse on a designated topic.

Among the practices described by the Greek sources were: a ritual wine libation and washing of the hands; the eating of various hors d'oeuvres before the main meal, including lettuce and various fruit and nut salads resembling our *haroset*, sometimes in the form of sandwiches (reminiscent of Hillel's famous custom); the singing of hymns to an assortment of gods, whose praises might make up the central topic of discussion; and the posing of a set of questions to set off the conversation.

Jewish tradition has typically given its own interpretations for these social conventions: Green vegetables symbolize the spring season, the *haroset* represents the mortar used by our enslaved forefathers, and so on. This ability to reinterpret foreign customs has always added to the strength and adaptability of Jewish tradition.

There is thus little doubt that the seder was consciously modeled upon the conventional Greco-Roman "formal dinner." In doing so however, the rabbis were laying themselves open to the danger that the borderline between the Jewish observance and the essentially pagan feast—which frequently had licentious or orgiastic dimensions—would be confused. An example of how they related to such problems can be found in the institution of the *afikoman*.

In current custom the *afikoman* is associated with a piece of matzah that the children steal in order to extort gifts from the adults, so that it can be eaten as the last item of the seder. In the Mishnah, though, it appears in a somewhat different context: "After the Passover offering, one should *not* end with *afikoman*." The reference is to a custom known as *epikomion*, a Greek word meaning "after dinner revelry" (related to the English word *comedy*). Normally this would involve going off to someone else's house, whether or not you have been invited, and indulging in another party.

What the Mishnah is saying is that, in spite of some of the apparent similarities between the seder and a pagan banquet, one should not treat it light-headedly as the Romans and Greeks would their own feasts. This meaning was understood by the rabbis of the Palestinian Talmud, who lived under Roman rule. By contrast, the Babylonian Talmud (whose authors lived farther away from the Greco-Roman world) came to understand the *afikoman* as a "dessert," translating the Mishnah as "One should not eat anything after the Passover *afikoman*."

Like many other Jewish customs, the Passover seder consists of a core of authentically Jewish traditions and values that were reformulated according to the concepts and vocabularies of different generations. As changes in culture and society made some of these observances strange and incomprehensible, Jewish tradition responded by supplying new interpretations.

It is through this approach of continually reinterpreting our past, that the tradition is saved from becoming obsolete.

What Is the Spiritual Symbolism of the Exodus?

P assover is of course the historical celebration *par excel-lence*, celebrating the formative event in Jewish history, the Exodus of the Israelites from Egyptian slavery. The events commemorated in this holiday have had continual relevance to Jew and gentile in all historical epochs, as a model for the understanding of their contemporary situations of national oppression, exiles, and liberations.

For many Jewish thinkers throughout the ages the lessons of Passover and the Exodus were not exhausted in their historical memories. The central themes that dominate the holiday were seen as metaphors and symbols for many facets of individual human psychology and religious experience.

THE MIXED MULTITUDE

A pioneer of this symbolic approach to reading the Bible was the first-century philosopher and exegete Philo Judaeus of Alexandria. For Philo the whole of Scripture was a complex mesh of symbols that illustrate the abstract truths and mysteries of philosophy and moral virtue. His treatment of the Exodus account is consistent with this approach.

147

In formulas that echo the assertion of the *Haggadah*, that "each individual must regard himself as if he himself had escaped from Egypt," Philo portrays "leaving Egypt" as an internal struggle that must be waged continually in every person's life. It is the fight to liberate one's mind from the temptations of the body, symbolized by Egypt, which is always trying to hold us back from the road leading to the freedom of virtuous living.

According to the biblical account, even after leaving Egypt the zeal of the Israelites was constantly being impeded by the "mixed multitude" among them, who would bewail their fate and longingly recall the fleshpots of Egypt. For Philo there is a "mixed multitude" in each of us, a part of the soul that remains under the dominion of the passions and irrational thinking. In the wicked this element exercises control.

The mind of the wicked man is indeed a "mixed multitude" of conflicting opinions, forever being pulled in opposing directions by the many false ideas that strive to lead him away from the single path of truth and goodness.

As in the case of the historical Exodus, the spiritual liberation from control of our irrational desires cannot be accomplished in a single moment. The contradictory directions of the mixed multitude keep us wandering in a confused wilderness instead of travelling the simple and direct route to religious fulfilment. According to Philo the very name "Passover" signifies that the true lover of wisdom is always practicing "passing over from the body and passions" in a quest to purify his soul.

REFINED IN EGYPT

The idea that Egypt is more than a geographical locale, but also represents a metaphysical state of impurity, has roots in talmudic literature. It is elaborated in the Jewish mystical tradition, in works such as the *Zohar*.

According to the *Zohar* the symbol of Egypt represents the "underside of wisdom" owing to its associations with magic and alchemy. The righteous must refine themselves by descending into the kiln of Egypt.

This is a pattern of spiritual development that dates back to Abraham, who had to sojourn in Egypt in order to test the strength of his newfound faith.

"It is the same [the *Zohar* concludes] with Abraham's children. When the Holy One wished to make them unique, a perfect people, and to draw them near to him—had they not gone down to Egypt and been refined there first—they would not have become his special ones."

RETURNING FROM EXILE

In treating the Passover story as a set of symbols, the Jewish commentators and homilies were not, of course, denying the historical truth of the events. In this they differed from many classical Christian writers for whom the symbolic meanings of texts would often supersede their literal sense. Nonetheless, the historical and allegorical interpretations seem to exist on separate, parallel, and mutually exclusive planes of meaning.

Some exegetes, however, were able to bridge this gap and dwell upon the close interconnections between visible history and the underlying spiritual levels. For Jews, it is argued, our fate as a nation is inevitably a reflection of the quality of our religious life.

This point was effectively demonstrated in a comment attributed to the Hasidic preacher Rabbi Jehiel Mikhal of Zlotchov.

Rabbi Mikhal was once approached by a student who was troubled by the wording of God's promise to Moses (Exodus 6:1) that Pharaoh would drive the Israelites out of Egypt "with a strong hand." Why, the student asked, should a slave who is being offered his freedom need to be forcibly driven out? Won't he run willingly from his slavery?

The rabbi answered that Israel's exile is always self-inflicted. Only when the Jews decide to release themselves can the demonic powers inside them be vanquished, and only then will the earthly rulers lose their power to subjugate Israel.

Concluded Rabbi Mikhal: Until the Israelites in Egypt declared themselves willing to return from spiritual exile, God was, as it were, powerless to help them. In the end, the sparks of holiness that were implanted in the enslaved Israelites awakened and were able to overpower the demonic forces of Egypt, which could not endure them any more, and proceeded to drive them out.

This is a message that would appear to have particular relevance in our generation, as the world seems to be bursting out in freedom and liberation. We have seen testimony that the human spirit can overcome political oppression; but on the other hand, we must remain aware that the achievement of political independence, in the absence of a true spiritual emancipation, is not the full realization of freedom.

How Does Passover
Celebrate Freedom?

In keeping with the Jewish cycle for the public reading of the Torah, the biblical account of the "Ten Plagues" was read just as the first volley of Scuds began to make their way toward Tel Aviv in January 1991.

It was eerie to reread the commands issued to the Israelites at the time: "None of you shall go out of the door of his house until the morning" (Exodus 12:22). As we chanted those verses, Israelis confined to their "sealed rooms" were praying that the agents of death would pass over them and leave them unscathed inside.

These events are typical of the innumerable ways in which the lives of Jews are given religious meaning through a reliving of the past. This feeling is most intense on Passover, "the season of our liberation."

For Jews, it is never enough merely to think of ideals like freedom or even to speak them; they must be acted on concretely as a part of life, even as Abraham's descendants had to suffer the bondage of Egypt before they could proclaim the ideal of human freedom.

At Passover each year we relive simultaneously the degradations of slavery and the exhilaration of freedom.

The bondage of Egypt influences much of biblical law: It is because we ourselves were "strangers in a strange land" that we must show sensitivity to the strangers among us, and it is because we experienced slavery that we must allow our dependents—and ourselves—a day of rest.

Perhaps the most surprising of these laws is where the Torah admonishes: "You shall not abhor an Egyptian, because you were a stranger in his land" (Deuteronomy 23:8). Even when fighting for your liberation you cannot forget the humanity of your enemy. Yet sympathy for the enemy does not cancel the obligation of fight tyranny.

The traditional Passover celebrations strive to maintain this difficult balance, expressing our joy over our deliverance, without gloating over the defeat of Pharaoh's armies. Accordingly, the Exodus from Egypt is celebrated on the first days of the festival with the singing of the full "Hallel" passage from Psalms, but on the final days, which commemorate the drowning of the Egyptians at the Red Sea, only a truncated version is recited, expressing the incompleteness of our joy.

Jewish legend describes how God Himself, while allowing the Israelites to celebrate in song their deliverance at the Red Sea, ordered the angels, who had not themselves known enslavement, to refrain from intoning God's praises in the face of the drowning Egyptians.

The Jewish ideal of a human (and never dehumanized) struggle for freedom is neither simple nor simplistic, and must be confronted anew in each generation. This is truly what Passover is about.

What Is the Significance of the Had Gadya?

The central precept of Passover is to transmit the message of the Exodus to our children. Our rabbis have traditionally invested much thought and energy into making sure that those children remain awake during the seder. Two of the most effective means toward this goal are the stealing of the *afikoman* and the rousing songs that are sung at the end of the evening.

At our house, there has never been much serious competition for the title of Favorite Seder Song. The award goes easily to the *Had Gadya*, which we sing to a lively variation on Moishe Oysher's brilliant mixture of klezmer and Dixieland tunes. The singing of the *Had Gadya* certainly provides a sufficient incentive for young and old alike to keep our eyes open, and a stirring jolt for anyone who might have nodded off by then.

Like several other songs that have found their way into the Haggadah, *Had Gadya* has no obvious connection to Passover, nor does it constitute an essential component of the liturgy. The current version first appeared in the Prague printing of the Haggadah in 1590 and its popularity was for a long time confined to Ashkenazic Jews. We are not very certain when, where, or why it was first composed, or even in what language. Like several other parts of the Haggadah, it is recited in Aramaic rather than Hebrew. According to one theory, though, it was originally written in Yiddish (in which language it appears in an old manuscript), and afterward translated into Aramaic in order to make it easier to imitate the Yiddish rhymes. Although this theory is supported by the poor quality of the Aramaic, other scholars have pointed out that Aramaic versions of the song are attested as far back as the thirteenth century in Avignon, in southern France, where Yiddish would not have been known.

The familiar version of the song begins with a cat eating a kid and culminates with God destroying the Angel of Death. There were, however, some interesting variations on this theme. In several versions it was a mouse—a rather formidable little rodent it would seem—who gobbled up the kid! In fact, the earliest text of the *Had Gadya* relates the sad story as an unending series in which "the cat came and ate the mouse who ate the rope that bound the ox who drank the water that extinguished the fire that burned the stick that beat the dog that ate the kid." The next page is missing in the manuscript, but it is likely that the cat went on to be devoured by the dog, setting the whole circle in motion again!

Although many modern scholars like to regard *Had Gadya* as no more than a frivolous bit of doggerel, analogous to such folk songs as "the House That Jack Built" or "the Farmer in the Dell," some of our rabbis, as well as several Christian writers, approached it with immense respect and tried to uncover its secret meanings. Most commentators saw it as a parable about Jewish history, in which one evil empire after another arises to oppress the defenseless Jewish "kid." This pattern will end in the messianic era, when God himself will do away with our oppressors and banish death.

The reverence in which the *Had Gadya* was held is exemplified by an incident that took place in the eighteenth century when a certain brash individual dared to make fun of the song and was immediately placed under a ban of excommunication by an irate observer. The episode was brought before the renowned Rabbi Hayyim Joseph David Azulai (known as the "Hida") who was thoroughly incensed that anyone should make light of a hymn that is recited by thousands of Jews and accepted by great rabbis. As evidence of the sanctity of the *Had Gadya*, the Hida tells of one eminent scholar who composed more than ten different commentaries to the song according to the different levels of mystical interpretation. The Hida, himself a seasoned kabbalist, entertained no doubts that the *Had Gadya* does indeed contain deep mysteries.

Whether your concern is to delve into its mystical dimensions or merely to keep your children alert during the seder, I hope you all have a wonderful time singing the *Had Gadya* this year.

Why Does Elijah
Visit the Seder?

S ince my childhood a special mystique has always been
generated by the presence at the Passover seder of a visitor who was never seen, but whose reality was no less tangible for that fact. The unseen guest is of course Elijah the
prophet. A special cup filled with wine was set for him, and
we all waited impatiently until the moment when one of us
would (often with discernible signs of fear at the prospect)
open the door to admit the righteous visitor. Our family dog
observed his own tradition of barking just before that moment as if he were greeting a more conventional caller. Afterward we would carefully measure Elijah's cup to verify that
the level of the wine had receded since being poured.

The belief that Elijah continues to wander about our
world is a mainstay of Jewish folklore. Rabbis in the Talmud were accustomed to running into him and addressing
questions to him about the goings-on in the Heavenly realms,
or about other matters that are normally concealed from
human view. Many tales were spun about how a ragged
vagrant was discovered, after his departure, to have been the
prophet in disguise, come to earth to test people's faith and
virtue, or to grant them a long-sought desire.

It is not hard to see how this role came to be assigned
to Elijah. The Bible relates how he was accustomed to travel

about assisting people in distress. He was also privileged to be numbered among the select few who never actually died; instead he was carried up to heaven in his lifetime in a flaming chariot. Elijah was thus eminently qualified to serve as an intermediary between the upper and lower worlds.

The original reason for opening the door probably had nothing to do with Elijah. The door opening occurs just after the conclusion of the meal and before the resumption of the Hallel, as we intone the words "Pour out thy wrath upon the nations that have not known thee, and upon the kingdoms that have not called upon thy name," a time when our European ancestors had good reason to check outside to make sure that there were no malevolent figures lurking outside ready to pounce upon the celebrants with accusations of the infamous blood libel that often ignited massacres of innocent Jews.

Another widespread belief held that Elijah's presence at the seder was necessary in order to resolve the talmudic dispute about how many cups of wine should be drunk that night, in keeping with the talmudic belief that certain facts remain undisclosed "until Elijah will come." The uncertainty grew out of the midrashic premise that the cups symbolized the four expressions of redemption contained in God's pledge to the enslaved Israelites: ". . . I will *bring you out* from under the burdens of the Egyptians, and I will *rid you out* of their bondage, and I will *redeem you* with a stretched out arm, and with great judgments. And I *will take you* to me for a people" (Exodus 6:6–7). Given this rationale, a doubt arose with regard to the words "And I will *bring you in* unto the land" in the next verse. Is it really appropriate to commemorate this promise, which was not to be fulfilled until after the generation of the Exodus had perished?

Talmudic tradition reports that Rabbi Tarfon advocated the drinking of a fifth cup. The two Babylonian academies of

Sura and Pumbedita were divided on this issue, as were several medieval Jewish communities. Some, like the Yemenites, have always included a fifth cup in their Haggadah. Rashi, on the other hand, was so opposed to the idea that he had Rabbi Tarfon's opinion excised from the talmudic manuscripts (which is why you will not find it in the printed editions of the Talmud).

Thus, the extra cup that is placed on the festive table, but is not drunk (at least not by the mortal participants) serves as a memorial to a practice that has been rejected by Ashkenazic Jews. It is understandable that this cup came to be identified with the name of the renowned resolver of halakhic doubts.

The two most prominent instances of the prophet's participation in the seder, the opening of the door and "Elijah's cup," have thus been seen to be relatively recent add-ons to the basic Passover service. There are, however, more substantial grounds for the widespread feeling that Elijah's spirit pervades the holiday and connects to its most essential themes and teachings.

Jewish tradition has always acknowledged a continuity between the past liberation of the enslaved Israelites and our future deliverance from the oppressions of exile. This attitude underlies the choice of the prophetic reading on the Sabbath preceding Passover, in which God offers his assurance that "I will send you Elijah the prophet before the coming of the great and dreadful day of the Lord." Because it is Elijah who will herald the advent of Messiah, Jews over the generations have clung tenaciously to the hope that the prophet would take advantage of his annual visits to Jewish households in order to proclaim the imminence of the cherished redemption.

Why Did American Jews Drink Raisin-Wine on Passover?

I don't know whether you prefer to use wine or grape juice to fulfill the requirement of drinking "four cups" at the Passover seder. For most of us this question is more a matter of personal taste than a strictly halakhic issue. This, however, has not invariably been the case, and several testimonies from and about American Jews in the middle of the nineteenth century tell us about a widespread opinion that unfermented "raisin-wine" was the only acceptable beverage for Passover use, and that alcoholic wine was severely frowned upon by Jewish tradition. Some even went so far as to say that alcoholic fermentation was included within the prohibition of *hametz*.

Now the preference for raisin-wine is not completely unreasonable. After all, commercially produced kosher wines were a rarity at this time, especially in America, so the only way to procure a ritually satisfactory beverage would be to make it at home. Though alcoholic wine cannot be easily manufactured by amateurs, raisin-wine can be prepared through a simple process of boiling the raisins in a pot. Admittedly, this was not strictly a Passover-related issue, but we all know how Jews often become especially meticulous in the observance of Pesah regulations even if they are lax about their dietary rules during the rest of the year.

We should also note that at this time a significant component of American Jews were descended from Sepharadic refugees, and that the consumption of homemade raisin-wine was a well-known Marrano practice, designed to avoid the drinking of Christian sacramental wines, at least on solemn religious occasions like Passover.

Whatever its origins, the Jewish preference for raisin-wine was to become a pivotal issue in the American public life of the era.

The latter half of the nineteenth century saw the rise of the Temperance Movement, which fought stubbornly for the limitation, or total prohibition, of intoxicating drinks. Although they were responding to a very real social problem in American society, the leaders of the Temperance agitation were drawn largely from the ranks of Evangelical Christians and were impelled by religious motivations. It was therefore a source of embarrassment to these Bible-thumpers that wine is mentioned so frequently in the Bible as the most common of beverages, to which no serious stigma or censure was attached. Even more painful to the Temperance cause was the story of the Last Supper where Jesus himself partook of wine and shared it with his disciples. According to the widespread view, the Last Supper had been a Passover seder.

Another commonly held view among Christians naively regarded contemporary Jews as faithful preservers of a fossilized tradition that had remained unchanged since Jesus' days. If it could be demonstrated that their Jewish neighbors drank non-alcoholic juice on Passover, then this could be considered conclusive evidence that the Bible itself was referring to the same beverage, and not to fermented wine.

The upshot of all this was that the American Christian world in the mid-nineteenth century developed a disproportionate interest in the Passover drinking preferences of their

Jewish compatriots, especially at the seder, and Christian tracts would contain frequent interviews with Jews—though not necessarily the most learned or observant of them. Even when the Jewish informants took care to distinguish between their personal practices and the customs of biblical Israel, the Temperance advocates had no qualms about quoting them selectively and out of context in order to prove their case.

American Jewish drinking habits were to take on a different significance after the Temperance lobby achieved its purposes and Prohibition became the law of the land in the United States. With the passing of the Eighteenth Amendment in January 1920, the government was authorized to issue special permits for religious and sacramental consumption of wine, and these permits became a valuable commodity during the "Roaring Twenties."

The proliferation of permit applications in the names of spurious Jewish "congregations" was given extensive coverage in the press, and the abuses (in which the criminal underworld sometimes had a hand) became a source of grave embarrassment to a Jewish community that was already under attack from anti-Semites and Nativist bigots.

Leaders of the Reform and Conservative movements responded by voluntarily forgoing their rights to permits, arguing that fermented wine was not really required by Jewish law. The Orthodox organizations did not follow suit, though they consistently declined to offer a halakhic justification for their position.

The wrath of the Orthodox organizations was to be ignited to even greater ferocity when the Reform leadership appealed to the American Internal Revenue Service, asking for a total repeal of the religious exemptions for *all* Jewish groups. At this point a new controversy split the Jewish community, as Jews from all denominations began to feel serious reservations about the Reformers' violation of the sacred separation of Church and State, and about their *chutzpah* in imposing halakhic positions upon Jews outside their own movement.

The divisions created by this controversy continued to affect Jewish communal life for a long time afterward.

Who Is an "Important" Woman?

O ne of the central themes of Passover is the idea that the liberation from Egypt has transformed all Jews—even those who are outwardly subjected to poverty or oppression—into free persons.

In order to give tangible expression to this fact, the ancient Rabbis modeled the seder after the formal banquets of the Roman nobility. At such occasions, the participants would recline luxuriously on their couches, enjoying the convivial conversation and nibbling on the hôrs d'oeuvres and delicacies arrayed before them.

A vestige of that practice is the custom of "leaning" on cushions around the table at our contemporary *sedarim*.

In connection with this practice, the Talmud states: "A women is not required to recline. However, if she is an important woman, then she must recline."

The traditional commentators and codifiers offer varying explanations as to why women should have been excluded from this expression of liberty.

A quick survey of these explanations can provide us with some instructive insights into the social and religious positions of women in different historical settings.

One of the earliest post-talmudic codes, an eighth-century collection of discourses known as the *She'iltot*, observed matter-of-factly that women were not accustomed to reclining at secular banquets. He does not provide us with a reason for this situation; perhaps the posture was considered immodest. In any case, since for women reclining did not serve as an expression of freedom on other occasions, it presumably followed that there would be no purpose served in requiring them to do so at the seder.

As we progress farther into the Middle Ages, attitudes and perspectives undergo some interesting changes. Several talmudic commentators now understand the women's exemption from reclining to be an extension of a wife's general subordination to her husband.

For instance, Rashi's grandson Rabbi Samuel ben Meir (known as "Rashbam"), writing in twelfth-century France, explained: "This is because a wife should be in awe of her husband and subject to his authority." A later French scholar, Rabbi Samuel of Falaise, concluded that it would be disrespectful for a wife to display authority or independence while in the presence of her husband.

Most authorities reasoned that if the exemption is understood to derive from the woman's relationship to her spouse, it followed that it would be in force only if he were actually present at the time. From this premise they went on to conclude that unmarried, widowed, or divorced women would be fully subject to the obligation to recline at the seder.

Some interpreters, such as the fourteenth-century Rabbi Manoah of Narbonne, formulated this position in more pragmatic and utilitarian terms: The rabbis exempted women from the requirement of reclining in order to allow them to devote their undivided attention to the preparation and serving of the food.

The differing rationales that were suggested to explain the women's exclusion from the obligation gave rise in turn to divergent definitions of the quality of "importance" that, according to the Talmud, would obligate women to recline at the seder.

Thus, those commentators who focused on the wife's being occupied in the kitchen would explain that an important woman is one who does not need to do her own housework, but can delegate the labor to servants (the sources do not contemplate the possibility of the husband cooking or serving the food).

Alternatively, Rabbi Eleazar Rokeah commented that if the key consideration is a wife's subordination to her husband, then the "important" woman would be one whose spouse is liberated enough not to object to her reclining.

There were some authorities who approached the concept of "importance" according to religious, rather than social, criteria. Thus, according to Rabbi Manoah, a woman who was the pious daughter of a distinguished scholarly family, embodying all the qualities of the Bible's "woman of valour"—"though no such paragon could actually exist—such a woman would be obliged to recline even if she were married!"

At any rate, the issue became moot when the majority of French and German Jewish authorities declared simply and categorically that "all our women are considered important, and they are therefore subject to the obligation to recline." This obligation was understood to apply equally to married and unmarried women, whether or not their husbands were present.

Why Did Some Jews
Dread Passover?

A passage in the Talmud records a grisly incident concerning a fatherless child who was left in the custody of his late father's family. The unfortunate lad was murdered by his guardians who stood to inherit his share in the estate of the deceased.

Subsequent Jewish law learned the lessons of this tragedy, decreeing that under such circumstances children should henceforth be assigned to the care of their mothers.

The original Talmudic report contained an indication of when the incident occurred. However, if one relies on the standard editions of the Talmud, the well-known Vilna printings produced at the beginning of the present century, it is hard to decipher what is being said there.

Where the date should appear, an ambiguous Hebrew abbreviation is employed, to which an anonymous marginal gloss comments: "This should be read as 'on the first evening,' and the printers of previous editions misinterpreted the abbreviation in a manner that is inappropriate to the context."

A comparison with earlier printings, manuscripts, and medieval citations makes it clear that the original reading of the phrase was "on Passover eve." The traditional commentators were somewhat puzzled over the importance of this detail. Some claimed that it was simply an incidental fact that had no particular significance to the legal or religious issues. Others suggested that the Talmud was emphasizing the perverseness of the crime, in that it was perpetrated at a time when Jews ought to be purifying themselves from corpse-related defilement in preparation for the pilgrimage to the Temple.

The question remains: Why did the recent editions of the Talmud take the trouble to alter the text and remove its connection to Passover?

My own initial investigation of this puzzle did not meet with immediate success. One leading contemporary talmudic scholar noted the emendation, adding cryptically that "many futile things have been written concerning the reading 'the eve of Passover,' none of which I consider satisfactory."

Indeed, it turns out that the "many futile things" were not written in the context of traditional talmudic commentaries, but relate to incidents that were taking place at the time of the printing of the Vilna Talmud editions.

In 1891 and 1892 a series of articles and pamphlets were published in German journals (including one with the transparent name *Antisemitische Corrospondenz*), from the pen of an individual named Augustus Rohling. These articles bore titles like "A Talmudic Source for Ritual Murder." In all these articles Rohling cited a garbled and distorted version of our talmudic passage as irrefutable evidence that Jews slaughter children—when necessary, even their own—as part of the religious observance of their Passover.

This absurd reading of the text was fully consistent with the other activities of Herr Rohling. He held the post of "Professor of Semitic Languages" at the German University in Prague, an appointment that owed more to pressures exerted by the church than to any legitimate academic credentials. His best known publication was the infamous *Der Talmudjude*, a vitriolic collation of twisted misquotes from Jewish sources (much of it plagiarized from earlier anti-Semitic anthologies) that claimed to prove the murderous character of Jews and Judaism. Rohling's rantings were cited in the prosecution of several European "Blood Accusations," including the notorious trial in Nyíregháza, Hungary, in 1883. Similar works are still in widespread circulation among his disciples in Alberta.

Rohling's pseudo-scholarship was repeatedly denounced and ridiculed by virtually all the contemporary Christian authorities on Hebrew and Jewish religion, including such distinguished experts as Hermann Strack, Franz Delitsch, and Theodor Nöldecke. Strack in particular, though an active missionary, had sufficient scholarly integrity and respect for the truth that he composed a special treatise to refute Rohling's slanders.

Eventually the wave of denunciations by a veritable who's who of European Orientalists, coupled with a series of lawsuits and countersuits, led to the anti-Semite's dismissal from his university post.

It is against the background of Rohling's dangerous libels, and the bloody pogroms that they were kindling in central and eastern Europe, that we can appreciate why the Jewish publishers tampered with the text of the Talmud in order to obscure its connections to Passover.

This can serve as a reminder of the days, unfortunately not completely bygone, when fear, rather than joyous anticipation, would often mark the approach of the "season of our liberation."

Who Staged the First Biblical Epic?

Cecil B. DeMille was not the first person to stage a dramatization of the Passover story.

Though it is impossible to ascertain who deserves that particular honor, we do know of a stage play based on the story of the Exodus that was composed as early as the second century B.C.E. The author of that play was a Jew named Ezekiel. As was the case with most of the cultural heritage that has survived from the illustrious Greek-speaking Jewish communities, Ezekiel's oeuvre was preserved by pagans and Christians, not by Jewish posterity.

"Ezekiel the Tragedian" entitled his drama the Exagogé (the *Exodus*). Arranged in five acts, it follows the career of Moses from his flight to Midian until after the revelation at Mount Sinai.

Ezekiel artfully blends a precise retelling of the biblical story with the literary conventions of Hellenistic culture. On the whole, he reflects the convictions of a proud Jewish community that their own sacred history was as worthy a subject for drama as the myths of their Greek and Roman neighbors.

Although the surviving remnants of the *Exagogé* testify to its faithful reliance on the Scriptural story, there are several apparent departures from the Bible that deserve our

attention. Some of these demonstrate the acceptance by
Hellenistic Jews of values and ideas that were current among
the Greeks and Egyptians.

For example, the play supplies details about Moses'
education that are not spelled out in the Torah. Not only was
he taught about his Jewish origins going back to Abraham,
but according to Ezekiel he also mastered the full range of
Egyptian wisdom. This detail is consistent with the opinion
that was widely held among the ancients—and by no means
limited to patriotic Egyptians—that Egypt was the birthplace of all true wisdom, and that such wisdom equipped
Moses ideally for the role of leader of his people.

Some of the most novel details in the *Exagogé* are those
that relate to its geographical setting.

Most of us have been brought up to assume that Midian,
to which Moses fled after killing the Egyptian taskmaster,
was somewhere on the Sinai Peninsula, as was Mount Sinai.
However, Ezekiel situates all these events on the African
mainland, in the Libyan region of Cyrene. This was an idea
that had considerable currency among ancient authors. The
Jewish historian Demetrius related that the descendants of
Abraham's wife, Keturah, believed to be the ancestors of
Moses' Midianite wife, Zipporah, had found their way to
Africa. Non-Jewish Hellenistic authors knew of many traditions related to the exploits of the African branch of Abraham's
descendants, including military and marital alliances with the
mighty Hercules.

In placing this unexpected emphasis on Cyrene as a
setting of formative Jewish history, the Hellenistic Jews were
emulating the attitudes of their Greek neighbors who maintained that North Africa was the cradle of civilization, and
associated it with many episodes in their mythical history,
from the journeys of Jason's Argonauts to the labors of Hercules. Indeed, it was believed that the Atlas Mountains housed

the primordial paradise of the Greek gods, a theme that may have influenced Ezekiel's idyllic portrayal of the biblical oasis of Elim (Exodus 15:27). It was only fitting that this cherished region should also have been the setting for the central events of Israelite history.

Another Greek mythological motif that Ezekiel incorporates into his drama was the legend of the marvelous phoenix, the bird whose rebirth out of the North African sands once in a millennium was believed to herald major historical epochs. Appropriately, the phoenix sighting is said to have occurred during the Hebrew Exodus, underscoring its importance as a historical turning point.

Some interesting twists in the dramatization emerge from the playwright's staging of the "burning bush" revelation. Here, the Jewish author found himself at a disadvantage vis à vis his pagan counterparts who could easily have actors play the roles of the various deities. Ezekiel, by contrast, had to represent a dialogue between Moses and an invisible God, an effect that he achieved by having the voice of God speak from behind curtains.

However Ezekiel's problem was not just a technical one. For a philosophically sophisticated Hellenistic Jew it was considered unacceptably crude to conceive of a spiritual God who literally possessed a "voice" in the human sense. Out of similar considerations, the renowned thinker Philo Judaeus of Alexandria reinterpreted many passages in the Bible that appeared to be referring to divine speech as mere metaphors designed to convey a process of intellectual perception.

Philo preferred to minimize God's direct involvement with the created world by applying the Stoic concept of the "Logos," an emanated entity that furnished the rational structure that regulates the physical world. In Philo's interpretations, it was this Logos, not God himself, that was heard or seen by the prophets of the Bible. This usage was adopted by the standard Aramaic translation of the Torah (where the Logos appears as the *memra*, the word of God) and continued to influence Jewish philosophers in later generations.

And so, while striving to fashion a literary representation of God's appearance to Moses, the tragedian Ezekiel was scrupulous in eschewing all references to the "voice" of God. Instead, he consistently makes reference to the "word of God," namely the divine "Logos," in a manner reminiscent of Philo.

You are probably asking yourselves: How was it possible in those primitive times before DeMille and Spielberg, to act out on a stage the miraculous splitting of the Red Sea? Ezekiel solved this problem by borrowing a trick that had previously been utilized by Aeschylus to dramatize the Battle of Salamis in *the Persians*. Instead of enacting the miracle directly, Ezekiel introduced the character of a lone Egyptian survivor who reported their calamity, in the most dramatic and graphic terms, to Pharaoh. In the surviving fragments of Ezekiel's scene, the Egyptian survivor gives us meticulous descriptions of the unequal array of forces, mounting gradually to the certainty that Egyptian victory is inevitable. When the tables are finally and suddenly turned in Israel's favor, it comes with overwhelming dramatic impact.

The many allusions in Ezekiel's play to its Cyrenian setting have led some scholars to believe that the author was himself a citizen of that region. If that theory is true, then it would provide a remarkable complement to several pieces of archeological evidence from that region that attest to the existence of a special amphitheater in Cyrene that was owned and utilized by the local Jewish community.

This invites some tantalizing speculations: Perhaps our synagogues should also give serious consideration to the introduction of theatrical dramatizations of biblical texts, as an alternative to some of our more longwinded preaching.

Why Is the Reed Sea Red?

The conclusion of Passover has traditionally focused on celebrating the miraculous parting of the Red Sea. There will certainly be some purists among my readers who are already jumping to correct me: The Hebrew *Yam Suf* should be rendered more precisely "the Sea of Reeds," a translation that has been adopted by some recent English biblical commentaries.

I have heard the accusation that the common English usage of "Red Sea" is nothing more than the result of the ignorance of early Bible translators, or perhaps an old typographical error. This is not the case at all.

Actually, the name "Red Sea" is a lot older than the English language, and can be traced at least as far back as the fifth-century B.C.E. Greek historian Herodotus. It is used standardly in the Septuagint, the oldest Greek translation of the Bible, and by Jewish writers such as Philo and Josephus Flavius.

If one reads these ancient authors one soon realizes that the body of water being referred to is not necessarily the one that currently bears that name. It seems to be applied to the entire maritime area between Africa, Arabia, and south Asia, extending at times as far as the Indian Ocean.

Some of the sources make a clear distinction between the more expansive Red Sea and the smaller Reed Sea. The latter lies in the region between Arabia and the Egyptian coast, especially in the Gulf of Eilat—the area that we normally think of now as the Red Sea.

It is likely that the Red Sea was so named by ancient sailors as a result of the peculiar coloring created by the mountains, corals, and desert sands (though the Egyptians called the same body of water the "Green Sea"); whereas the "Reed Sea" takes its name from the papyrus reeds and bulrushes that proliferated along the nearby Nile.

The distinction between the two seas is made very clearly in a remarkable document preserved among the Dead Sea Scrolls that is known to scholars as the "Genesis Apocryphon." This Aramaic text retells the stories of the Hebrew Patriarchs, much of it presented as an autobiographical account narrated by Abraham himself.

In one episode, Abraham tells us how he travelled along the frontier of the land that God had promised him, progressing from the Gihon River (apparently identified with the Nile), to the Mediterranean, south Lebanon, and along the Euphrates River. Following that river through what is now Iraq, Abraham arrived at the Red Sea in the east, which he traced through to "the tongue of the Reed Sea, which goes forth from the Red Sea."

From this itinerary it is evident that the Reed Sea is an inlet of the Red Sea. The fact that Abraham reached the Red Sea from the mouth of the Euphrates shows us that what is being referred to is in fact none other than the Persian Gulf!

The implications are quite remarkable. While I do not believe that we necessarily have to begin speaking of the "miraculous parting of the Persian Gulf," it is intriguing to observe that the story places both Iraq and Saudi Arabia within the perimeters of the Promised Land, a view that will warm the hearts of the most extreme Israeli right-wingers.

As for myself, I will be perfectly satisfied if people simply stop correcting me whenever I speak of "the Red Sea."

THE OMER SEASON

Why Was Judaism Split over the Counting of the Omer?

The period between Passover and the festival of Shavu'ot is designated the Omer according to the biblical precept (Leviticus 23:10–16) that commands "you shall bring a sheaf (omer) of the first fruits of your harvest unto the priest. And he shall wave the sheaf before the Lord to be accepted for you."

The sheaf (traditionally understood to be of barley, whose harvest generally occurs by Passover) is to be "waved before the Lord," with accompanying sacrifices, and only after this ceremony may the grain of the new year be consumed.

Subsequently the Torah outlines the following procedure (verse 15): "And you shall count for yourselves from the morrow after the Sabbath from the day that you brought the sheaf of the wave-offering; seven Sabbaths shall be complete," until, on the fiftieth day, the Festival of Weeks (Shavu'ot) is celebrated with its distinctive sacrifices and rituals.

Contemporary observance of this precept excludes, for obvious reasons, those elements of the rite that are dependent on the existence of the Jerusalem Temple. Nevertheless, the rabbis of the Talmud understood that the practice of counting seven weeks is binding even in generations that cannot actually wave the sheaf. Thus, traditional Jews still continue to count each night the number of days that have elapsed since the day when their ancestors would have offered up the omer in the Temple precincts.

BEGINNING THE COUNT

When does this count begin? The verse that we quoted designates the "morrow after the Sabbath" as the time for waving the sheaf. Understood literally, this would imply that the count must invariably begin on the same day of the week: a Sunday. (*Which* Sunday is far from clear. Perhaps during Passover, perhaps the one immediately following, or maybe the first one after the ripening of the barley crop.)

Similarly, the count would *end* on a Sunday, and Shavu'ot would invariably fall on the same day of the week, though not on a designated calendar date (thus in verse 16: "Even until the morrow after the seventh Sabbath shall you count fifty days").

Anyone who is familiar with actual Jewish practice knows that this is not the way the calculations are actually done. The counting of the omer invariably begins on the second night of Passover, on whichever day of the week that might happen to fall, and concludes with Shavu'ot, always on the sixth day of the Hebrew month of Sivan.

"Sabbath" was understood by the rabbis as referring, in the first instance, to the first day of Passover (on which most classes of labor are forbidden); and in the second, to the week as a whole (that is, "after the conclusion of the last week of the count"; this is a normal usage in rabbinic Hebrew).

And in fact we find that the question of the dating of the omer ritual was a source of major conflict among the Jewish sects and movements of the Second Temple era, some of whose implications we have begun to understand only recently.

THE COUNT CONFLICT

The tradition that *sabbath* really means "festival" is an ancient one, and was utilized in the Septuagint, the third century B.C.E. Greek translation of the Torah commissioned by King Ptolemy Philadelphus of Egypt. The Septuagint is generally a literal translation, and its occasional departures from literalism can often serve as a warning sign that something is afoot.

Talmudic literature records a number of controversies with a sect known as the *Baitusim*, a little-known Second Temple religious movement. These controversies focus precisely on this question.

The *Baitusim* insisted on counting from Sunday, and in order to prevent the Pharisees from counting from the first day of Passover they would do everything in their power to confuse the issue, including trying to deceive the Sanhedrin (the Supreme Court, sitting in Jerusalem) by misrepresenting the date of the New Moon (which, in those days, was determined not according to a fixed calendar, but by the testimony of witnesses who had seen the renewal of the moon), or by sending out false signals (at that time the New Moon was announced through the lighting of a chain of bonfires) about which date had been determined as the New Moon.

These *Baitusim* were concerned in particular that the harvesting of the omer sheaves should not fall on a Sabbath. For the Pharisees, this was a possibility and in their view the biblical command would override the normal prohibition against harvesting on Saturday. For their opponents harvesting on the wrong day was an unjustifiable desecration of the Day of Rest.

The Mishnah records special rituals for the harvesting of the omer on the Sabbath, in which great emphasis was laid on the publicity of the event. Each act was described loudly three times, proudly asserting that it was in fact Shabbat, and that nonetheless they were harvesting the sheaf. All this was done in order to emphatically dissociate themselves from the literalism of the *Baitusim*.

Talmudic literature tells us very little about the ideology or motivations of the *Baitusim*, other than the literalistic approach to the biblical text that they shared with several other movements in the Jewish world.

A new perspective was added to our understanding of the phenomenon when scholars began to compare the rabbinic writings with the Book of Jubilees, an unusual volume composed probably during the second century B.C.E. and claiming to record a revelation to Moses by the "Angel of God's Presence." It retells the narratives of the Torah according to its own peculiar ideology.

One of the most important themes of the Book of Jubilees is that, contrary to traditional Jewish custom, the Bible commands us to use a solar calendar of 364 days a year. Since the number 364 is evenly divisible by seven, it turns out that all the festivals will fall on fixed days of the week. According to their view, the counting is to begin on the Sunday immediately following Passover.

When the Dead Sea Scrolls were discovered in the 1940s it was noted that the sect who had produced the scrolls observed the "Jubilees calendar," and accepted Jubilees as a canonical work. The fact that they operated according to a different calendar has been seen as one of the main reasons why they were forced to withdraw to their hermit-like community in the Judean desert.

Some scholars pointed out that in manuscripts the word *Baitusin* usually appears as two words: *beit sin* (the house of Sin); and the suggestion was proposed that perhaps this is the original Hebrew form for the name that was preserved in Greek sources as "Essenes," a group described at length by ancient writers as living a secluded communal existence in the Judean wilderness, identified by many scholars with the Dead Sea sect, but apparently not mentioned by name in the whole of rabbinic literature. Indeed, the *Baitusim* are linked in the Talmud with Ma'aleh Adumim, on the way to the Dead Sea.

The issue of the dating of the omer period is thus seen to be not an isolated halakhic dispute, but an instance of a basic divergence of approaches to Jewish observance.

Our knowledge of this episode took on fascinating new dimensions with the publication by Professor Yigael Yadin in the 1970's of the Temple Scroll, one of the most important of the Dead Sea writings.

In addition to the reliance on the 364–day calendar, common to the other scrolls, the Temple Scroll revealed before us an entire series of some four different forty-nine-day "countings," extending throughout the summer months, each one terminating in a different festival of agricultural thanksgiving, not only for the barley, but also for the wheat, wine, and (olive) oil. The centrality of the omer question to the worldview of the sect is thus seen to be more far-reaching than we had hitherto imagined, and it will probably be some time before we can understand its full significance.

ORAL LAW DOCTRINE

Why did the Pharisaic-rabbinic tradition reject the simple literal interpretation of the biblical text?

Actually, the rabbis argue at length that their interpretation is the correct rendering of the passages in Leviticus, though their arguments are far from convincing. Such traditions are generally seen as an example of the "doctrine of the oral Law," the characteristic ideology of the rabbis that states that the written Torah is not complete in itself, but must be modified and complemented by a living tradition transmitted by the authoritative interpreters in each generation.

In our instance, perhaps another factor is to be discerned as well. By beginning the count from the second day of Passover, we discover that the festival of Shavu'ot coincides with the day on which the Torah was given at Mount Sinai. It thus allows the transformation of the Feast of Weeks from a purely agricultural festival into a historical one which commemorates one of the central events in Israel's history.

This understanding of Shavu'ot appears to be a typical "Oral Law" innovation of rabbinic Judaism, audaciously adding a new dimension of meaning to the tradition. Ironically, the commemoration of the giving of the *written* Torah can only be observed if we accept the dating supplied by the *oral* Law tradition.

The study of Jewish history and traditions is still a vibrant endeavor, and further discoveries promise to add new insights into an ancient heritage.

Why Do We Mourn during the Omer season?

It is now the almost universal practice among traditional Jews to observe the season of counting the omer as a time of sadness, by refraining from activities that are associated with gaiety and celebration. The mourning period lasts from Passover until the thirty-third day, known as La"g ba'omer.

The melancholy mood of the omer season is usually linked to the well-known talmudic tradition about how thousands of Rabbi Akiva's students perished between Passover and Shavu'ot. The Babylonian Talmud states that they died of a plague, though many historians discern a reference to death in battle, in the ill-fated Bar Kokhba revolt (in 135) of which Rabbi Akiva was an active supporter.

The earliest records we possess about mourning during the omer are contained in the Responsa of the Babylonian *Ge'onim*, who observed the restrictions during the entire forty-nine-day period, with no respite on the thirty-third day. The only prohibitions that are enumerated in these early texts are the holding of weddings and doing work after nightfall. Not until the thirteenth century was the list augmented to include shaving and cutting the hair.

The cessation of mourning practices on La"g ba'omer is not mentioned before the twelfth century in Spain and southern France, and the original significance of this date remains shrouded in obscurity. The shortening of the period was justified by means of an ingenious new interpretation of the talmudic passage about the deaths of Rabbi Akiva's disciples, according to which the plague had come to a halt half a month before Shavu'ot, just after the thirty-third day of the omer.

The new practice and its historical rationale were accepted by most of the Sepharadic halakhic authorities, including the *Shulhan Arukh*. It is now followed by Jewish communities throughout the world.

Examination of early texts reveals that the older practice among Ashkenazic Jews was somewhat different from its current form. Instead of excluding the last third of the omer period from the mourning observances, the Jews of medieval Germany used to commence the mourning customs two weeks into the omer—at the beginning of the month of Iyyar—and continued them all the way through to Shavu'ot.

The reasons for the special character of the omer season among Ashkenazic Jews becomes evident when we survey some of their synagogue rituals. From the beginning of Iyyar they would include special liturgical poems (*piyyut*) in commemoration of local massacres, and a memorial prayer for the souls of martyrs was recited on the Shabbat preceding Shavu'ot. This last-mentioned prayer was the familiar Av Harahamim text that we still read on most Saturdays, and it is for this reason that we recite it during the omer season even on festive Sabbaths (such as when Rosh Hodesh is announced), although it would have been omitted on equivalent occasions at other times of the year.

In the Ashkenazic custom, the intensity of the mourning was also increased by forbidding additional activities, such as wearing new clothing, bathing for pleasure, and trimming fingernails.

It is possible to identify with precision the tragic events that were being commemorated by these practices. In the year 1096, bloodthirsty bands of Crusaders marched through the Rhine basin, mercilessly slaughtering Jewish men, women, and children. The worst bloodshed occurred between the first of Iyyar and Shavu'ot. The Jewish populace of Speyer was attacked on the eighth of Iyyar, and the illustrious communities of Mainz and Köln fell to the marauders during the week preceding Shavu'ot.

It is hardly surprising that subsequent generations of Ashkenazic Jews came to focus their grief on the massacres that had occurred during that time of the year.

As always, our Jewish religious calendar maintains a living link between ourselves and the Jews of earlier eras. The rhythms of the omer period, originating in the joys of the harvest and the associations with Passover and Shavu'ot, were transformed into monuments to national tragedy during the Bar Kokhba revolt and the Crusades. In recent times we have forged our own links to this living historical chain, by setting aside days to commemorate the momentous events of our times, the Holocaust, and the sacrifices of Israel's soldiers, as well as the elation of renewed Jewish statehood and the return to Jerusalem.

ISRAELI
INDEPENDENCE DAY

Were There Really Two Thousand Years of Exile?

"To be a free people in our own land," proclaim the inspiring words of Israel's anthem, the *Hatikvah*, "is the hope of two thousand years." I admit that I find the phrase very puzzling. The magic number of two thousand years is one that has become an ubiquitous cliché in Israeli conversation, where it is not at all strange to hear proud references to achievements like "the first Israeli basketball championship in two thousand years," and so forth.

Interestingly, the original lyrics of the Zionist anthem as composed by the poet Naftali Hertz Imber did not specify the age of the hope, speaking merely of an "ancient hope." The fact that the two thousand years did get interpolated onto the text bears witness to how central that number has come to be in Jewish consciousness.

What is the real significance of that time definition? In my experience, it has invariably been used to indicate a rough approximation of the time that has elapsed since the destruction of the Second Temple by the Romans in 70 C.E. No doubt that was a national tragedy of terrible proportions involving not only the death, destruction, and suffering of a viciously suppressed rebellion, but also a traumatic crisis in religious life as the Jews found themselves without the sanctuary that had hitherto stood at the center of their worship.

There might have been more justification for using the phrase if its starting point had been in 63 B.C.E. when the Roman conquest of Jerusalem under Pompei brought a formal end to a century of Hasmonean sovereignty. In actual practice, however, it is the year 70 that is always singled out in the popular Jewish memory as the turning point in our political destiny. As one widely used Jewish history text puts it: ". . . Jerusalem fell and the Temple went up in flames. The Jewish state had ceased to be." In truth, at the time of this disaster, Judea had not been an independent Jewish state for well over a century.

As noted above, the words of the *Hatikvah* seem to imply that the destruction of the Temple marked the beginning of Jewish exile as well as statelessness. Though this perception seems to be a very widely held one, it is also devoid of factual foundation.

Jewish exile is a phenomenon that dates back many centuries before 70 C.E., to the captivity of the "ten lost tribes" of the northern Israelite monarchy, which was to be followed by the destruction of Judea and the first Temple, when masses of Jews were exiled to Babylonia.

When the Jews returned to their homeland under Ezra and Nehemiah in the sixth century B.C.E., it was only a small group of loyalists who were prepared to leave their now-comfortable existences in Babylonia. The majority were of a less pioneering spirit, electing to remain in exile. Even those who did return to Jerusalem did not enjoy political independence, but passed through the hands of an assortment of foreign governments—Persian, Ptolemaic, and Seleucid—until the successful rebellion of the Maccabees and the brief period of independence that ensued.

Through all periods of subsequent Jewish history there were more Jews living outside the borders of the Holy Land than within. The destruction of the Second Temple did not change that fundamental situation, though it did result in the expulsion of additional numbers of Jews, many of whom were taken as slaves to Rome.

Another version of the argument would have it that the significance of the two thousand years lies in the fact that from 70 c.e. the land of Israel became almost emptied of its Jews. This is also an absurd notion. Literary and archeological evidence attest to the fact that Jews continued to be the dominant population in most regions of Palestine for many centuries afterwards.

This fact is amply demonstrated by the monumental literary creations of the era: the Mishnah, the Palestinian Talmud, and a rich assortment of other rabbinic works. It is also apparent in the dozens of synagogues and other monuments to thriving Judaism that are continually being unearthed in Judaea and the Galilee.

The more we learn about our past, the longer we find that Palestinian Jews maintained a vibrant religious and cultural life. Not too long ago it was commonly held that Jewish life functionally disappeared from the region from the fourth century with the advent of Constantine and the Christianization of the Roman Empire. Under the severe persecutions—so the theory argued—many Jews abandoned their homeland, and those who remained were unable to produce anything of lasting value.

This view has also been discarded in the face of the historical data. It was precisely during this period of persecution that Jews in the Land of Israel were producing some of the most impressive creations of Jewish literary history: the many volumes of midrashic commentaries to the Bible, the masterpieces of liturgical poetry, the intensive study of the text and language of the Bible (Masora), and much more.

An interesting by-product of this situation was noted at the beginning of the revival of Jewish settlement in Israel in this century. When names had to be assigned to Jewish settlements it often proved surprisingly simple to reconstruct the original Hebrew name of the place, because it had been preserved in the Arabic. This simple phenomenon is actually of profound importance. When the Arabs conquered Palestine in the seventh century, many of these localities actually bore "official" Greek names. The Arabs, however, did not use the Greek names, but the ones they picked up from their current inhabitants, who were mostly Jews. They, of course, referred to their villages by their original Hebrew names.

I suspect that the myth of two thousand years of Jewish exile owes much of its popularity to its use by Christians. For them there was a theological import to asserting that the Jewish situation was radically changed soon after the time of Jesus as a punishment for their rejection of him. This argument figures prominently in ancient polemics, and has apparently penetrated into the Jewish consciousness as well.

As it relates to the later periods (between the third and tenth centuries), it seems that there were Jewish parties who had their own motives for minimizing the achievements of Palestinian Jewry. This era was marked by a fierce rivalry between the rabbinic leaderships of Babylonia and the Land of Israel for dominance in the religious life of world Jewry. It was the Babylonians who ultimately prevailed, largely because they had the support of the major superpower of the time, the Muslim Caliphate centered in Baghdad (which now became the home of the major talmudic academies of the region).

This rivalry often expressed itself in intensely polemical utterances in which Babylonian Jews would try to delegitimize the traditions of their Palestinian cousins, arguing that the latter's customs were not to be taken seriously because they were nothing more than emergency measures adopted during times of persecution. The "persecution" theory proved very convenient, since it allowed the Babylonian rabbis to reject Palestinian traditions without actually showing overt disrespect for the revered citizens of the Holy Land.

A similar phenomenon arose in modern times with the rise of the Zionist movement and the State of Israel. Israeli curricula in Jewish history (especially in the secularist stream) tend to skip directly from the Bar Kokhba revolt in the second century to the rise of Zionism at the end of the nineteenth. Everything in between is an uninteresting saga of persecution and oppression that is the antithesis of the Zionist ideal. This image of two thousand years of Jewish passivity served the ideological interests of Zionism as well, by equating geographical dispersion with political power-lessness. The fact that a number of short-lived independent Jewish states did arise in various places during the Middle Ages, outside the Land of Israel, is another story altogether, and would make an interesting subject for a separate study.

For the moment it strikes me as a bit too late in the game to emend the accepted lyrics of the *Hatikvah*. But I shall always feel uncomfortable singing that line.

JERUSALEM
REUNIFICATION DAY

Can a Palestinian Folktale
Become a Midrash?

T he following story is probably familiar to most of my
readers. I have heard it told on innumerable occasions
from the pulpits of synagogues in Israel and the Diaspora.

According to the tale, there long ago lived two brothers
who shared a field and whose crops they used to divide
equally. One of the brothers was a bachelor, and the other a
married man with many children. Once, during the harvest,
each of them felt pity for the other. The bachelor was wor-
ried that his brother did not have enough to feed his household, while the married brother had concern for his brother's
solitude. In the dark of the night each of them would carry
some sheaves of produce to the other's house, and in the
morning each would be astonished to discover that their own
supplies had not diminished. This went on for several days
and nights until the two finally met tearfully during one of
their nocturnal errands. At that point it was decreed from
above that this was the place upon which it would be fitting
to establish God's Holy Temple.

The rabbis who tell this moving story, often in connection with Jerusalem day, usually cite it as a talmudic legend taken from the "midrash." Making allowances for the
limitations of my own erudition, I was always troubled that
I had not encountered the story of the two brothers in any

of the standard compendia of rabbinic lore. As it turns out, the same problem had troubled a more capable scholar than myself, the late Professor Alexander Scheiber of Budapest, who devoted a number of special studies to the history of the legend.

According to Scheiber's researches, the earliest attestation of the story appears in the writings of Alphonse de Lamartine, a noted French author with an affection for the Bible and its land. He claims to have heard it from the mouth of an Arab peasant during a journey through the Holy Land in 1832. The literary record of that journey was published in 1835.

From that point on, versions of the tale began to appear in several European languages, including German and Hungarian. It also found its way into Jewish writings, such as the moralistic anthology, *Mikveh Yisra'el*, by Rabbi Israel Costa of Livorno, Italy, which was published in 1851 and a collection of miracle tales (*Ma'aseh Nissim*) that was printed in Baghdad around the turn of the century.

The story has become so familiar that many knowledgeable Jews are convinced that it is indeed a talmudic *Aggadah*. Some have insisted that the Arabs might be preserving an originally Jewish tradition that for some reason was not recorded in our own literature.

The fact is that even in ancient times it was not uncommon for foreign legends and fables to find their way into the volumes of talmudic and midrashic teachings. Our rabbis did not live in isolation from their surroundings, and recognized that an edifying teaching is worth retelling no matter what its source. The concept of "midrash" is accordingly a dynamic one, and there is nothing inherently novel or unacceptable about receiving an Arab folk-tale into the family of Jewish legend. Indeed, the story of "the two brothers" accurately reflects the traditional reverence that Islam has always held for the site of the *Bait al-muqdasah* (the Temple) and its builder, King Solomon. The story, by the way, is still part of the living oral tradition of the Palestinian Arabs.

The main purpose of the legend was to emphasize the values of peace, compassion, and brotherly love that are symbolized by Jerusalem and the Temple. Is it not, therefore, doubly appropriate that in admitting (or repatriating) this story into Jewish tradition we should have to express a debt of gratitude precisely to those cousins with regard to whom it has been so difficult to realize those very ideals!

SHAVU'OT

Who Was Obadiah
the Proselyte?

The festival of Shavu'ot is the day on which Judaism honors its converts. This theme is most pronounced in the reading of the book of Ruth, which relates the story of how a Moabite woman chose to cast her lot in with the Jewish people and was destined to become the great-grandmother of King David.

We do not usually think of ourselves as a missionizing people. During the Middle Ages, when Jews lived precariously under the heavy yokes of Christianity and Islam, the seeking of converts could be a perilous undertaking. And yet, in spite of the severe penalties that were sometimes inflicted upon both the converts and the communities that accepted them, Judaism never ceased to attract a small but steady stream of proselytes.

In this article I would like to speak of one such proselyte, a figure who lived in Italy during the eleventh century. The individual in question only came to the attention of scholars during the last generations, as fragments of a detailed biographical chronicle were pieced together from the tattered manuscripts of the Cairo *Genizah*.

The chronicle tells of a young Norman priest named Johannes whose study of the Bible gradually convinced him that it was the Jews who faithfully continued the ways of

205

the ancient Hebrews. Johannes was also an eyewitness to the First Crusade and was impressed at how heroically Jews faced the murderous attacks of the rampaging Crusaders. He had heard of the Italian archbishop Andreas of Bari who had adopted Judaism, a decision that forced him to flee to Constantinople to escape the wrath of his former coreligionists. Inspired by Andreas' deeds, Johannes took on the Hebrew name Obadiah and set to wandering among the Jewish communities of the Middle East.

The name Obadiah seems to have been reserved for proselytes. This accords with the talmudic tradition that states that the biblical prophet of that name had been a convert. A different Obadiah the Proselyte, who lived somewhat later, was the recipient of a famous responsum by Maimonides.

Obadiah's chronicle is a source of extraordinary glimpses into events of the time. He describes the battles of the Crusaders and the sufferings of the civilians in besieged cities. He tells of the beginnings of the first discriminatory laws that were imposed on the Jews of Aden (including heavy taxes and distinguishing dress regulations).

One theme that recurs constantly in Obadiah's chronicle is the intense messianic fervor that pervaded the times. No fewer than three self-styled Jewish messiahs are mentioned in the brief fragment. The Jews of the time, no doubt sensing that the war between the Christians and the Muslims must have cosmic significance, placed their complete faith in these pretenders, and after the hoped-for redemption failed to materialize they became a laughingstock to their Muslim neighbors.

One of Obadiah's writings holds a special fascination for us. It preserves a set of liturgical poems that he had heard in the synagogues, and that he had recorded according to the precise system of musical notation that was in use among

Christian Europeans, but which was as yet unknown to Jews. It is perhaps more than coincidental that one of these poems was composed for Shavu'ot. Several years ago I had occasion to hear it performed in concert in Jerusalem, and it was a powerful feeling to hear these lost voices chanting from out of the Jewish past.

No less impressive is the glimpse that Obadiah gives us into daily lives of the Jewish communities among which he lived. Whether in Baghdad or Damascus, Israel or Egypt, the new convert was invariably welcomed by the local Jews, who would give him food, shelter, and religious schooling, in spite of the difficult circumstances to which they were subjected.

What was the Shavu'ot Divorce Controversy?

Owing to delays in notifying distant Jewish communities about the date when the new month had been declared in Jerusalem, extra days were added to what were originally supposed to be single-day festivals. Traditional Jews outside of Israel continue to observe the second days of the holidays even though their original reason became anachronistic with the adoption of a permanent calculated calendar.

There are, in fact, several exceptions and anomalies to the practice. For example, Rosh Hashanah is observed even in Israel for two days, whereas a two-day Yom Kippur fast was (thankfully) not considered a feasible option.

There is also an intriguing inconsistency in the observance of a second day of Shavu'ot, since the date for this holiday is not determined according to the day of the month, but by the counting of the omer for fifty days after the first day of Passover. Thus, even in ancient times, there would never have arisen any doubts about the correct date of Shavu'ot.

Nonetheless, the halakhic tradition decided to add a second day in order to maintain consistency among the various holidays.

Under normal circumstances, the questionable status of the second day of Shavu'ot would not entail any practical consequences.

I recall, for example, the time when I was serving with the Israeli army in Lebanon and we were allowed to go home for Shavu'ot. I tried to persuade my commanding officer that, since we were outside of Israel, we were entitled to two days' leave. It is to the credit of Tzahal that they were not taken in for a moment by my specious argument.

On a much more serious level, the status of the second day of Shavu'ot was the focus of a nineteenth-century controversy, which became a cause célèbre throughout the Jewish world.

The story involved a man in the Galician town of Brody who had taken ill and was deemed to have only hours left to live. The man had no children, and therefore his widow would become subject to the biblical law of levirate marriage. This meant that she would be unable to remarry unless she obtained a formal release from her late husband's brother, through the ceremony of *halitzah*. Since her brother-in-law lived in Italy, this would be difficult to accomplish, rendering the unfortunate widow an *agunah*, an "anchored woman." Out of consideration for his wife's fate, the husband proposed to divorce her in the last remaining hours of his life.

Unfortunately the timing of the events was problematic. It was Shavu'ot, when it would normally be forbidden to write a *get*. When the case was brought before the local halakhic authority, the eminent Rabbi Eleazar Landau, he cited the far-reaching leniencies that the halakhah had often adopted in order to ease the burden of the *agunah*, and ruled that in the present circumstances concern for the potential suffering of a widow should override the flimsy basis of the second day of Shavu'ot. He ordered that a scribe be brought on the second day and that the divorce be duly issued.

Not everyone was pleased with Rabbi Landau's decision. A distinguished local sage, Rabbi Solomon Kluger,

objected to his colleague's tampering with an accepted Jewish
ritual, and appealed to Rabbi Moses Schreiber of Pressburg
(today's Bratislava), the renowned "Chasam Sofer" who was
considered that generation's most distinguished spokesman
for traditionalist Judaism.

The Chasam Sofer had often marshalled his phenomenal scholarship in an unrelenting war against the Enlightenment and Reform movements, opposing any innovations
that might challenge or weaken the authority of traditional
Judaism and the rabbis who upheld it.

The Chasam Sofer argued that the very fact that the
second day of Shavu'ot could not be justified on normal
grounds showed that it was an independent rabbinic law,
and not just a consequence of calendrical doubts. Basing
himself on a talmudic principle that rabbinic ordinances
must be defended more firmly than those of the Torah itself, he argued that any diminishing of the status of the second day of Shavu'ot would invite further challenges to the
authority of the rabbinic tradition, and eventually lead to a
complete erosion of Judaism.

In the animated and often vitriolic controversy that
ensued, it was the position of the Chasam Sofer that eventually gained the upper hand, and is most frequently cited
by Orthodox authorities.

I admit that I find it easier to sympathize with the situation of the unfortunate widow, and with Rabbi Landau's
humane subordination of ritual to ethical considerations.
However, we must also appreciate the position of Rabbi
Schreiber in its historical context. The Chasam Sofer was
waging a desperate campaign against forces that, in his view,
threatened the very survival of Judaism. The experience of
the German Enlightenment, which over two short generations had brought about a massive defection from the Jewish ranks, certainly provided legitimate grounds for alarm;

and the feared liberal ideologies had already made significant inroads in Brody, the scene of our controversy, which
was strategically situated on the border between central and
eastern Europe.

The issues that underlay the dispute are still too fresh
for us to dispassionately apply the insights of historical hind-
sight. In the long run, we cannot yet judge whether the interests of Jewish continuity were best served by the intran-
sigence of the Chasam Sofer or by the flexibility of Rabbi
Landau in their differing attitudes toward the second day
of Shavu'ot.

Why Do We Decorate the Synagogue with Greenery on Shavu'ot?

The tradition of decorating synagogues and homes with greenery on Shavu'ot has a long history. As a characteristic observance of Ashkenazic Jews, it is described by Rabbi Jacob Möllin (the "Maharil"), the foremost medieval authority on German-Jewish traditional practice. With some variations, it was also observed among Jews in Italy, Egypt, Persia, and other localities.

The origins of the custom are shrouded in obscurity, and the commentators were at a loss to find a definitive explanation.

There is no obvious link between the greenery and Shavu'ot's most prominent theme of the revelation of the Torah at Mount Sinai. Nevertheless Rabbi Moses Isserles, citing the practice in his glosses to the *Shulhan 'Arukh*, asserted cryptically that the purpose of the decorations is indeed to recall the joy of the giving of the Torah.

The ingenuity of later commentators was harnessed to the task of uncovering the symbolic link between that event and the floral ornamentation.

In their quest for an explanation, several writers draw our attention to Exodus 34:3, in which God forbade the Israelites to graze their flocks on the mountainside. This prohibition, argued our commentators, would have been superfluous unless Mount Sinai was adorned with green pasturage—as it is indeed depicted in some Hebrew manuscript illuminations. Ergo, our custom of adorning the synagogues with grass must be a recollection of the theophany at Mount Sinai!

Other authorities suggested more symbolic associations. Some recalled that the fragrant blossoms and herbs of the Song of Songs are traditionally viewed as allegories for the sweet words of Torah; and the people of Israel who accepted it on this day were likened to God's private and protected orchard.

A more tangible connection between the revelation at Sinai and the floral realm is suggested in a midrashic manuscript first published some fifty years ago. The author's point of departure is the Bible's singling out of the *third* day of the people's encampment as the time when the Almighty descended upon Mount Sinai. This calls to mind the third day of the Creation, when the earth put forth grass and fruit trees. The similarity is seen to be a significant one: Just as fruit is essential for physical life, so the Torah is no less vital for our spiritual sustenance: "It is a tree of life for all who take hold of it."

If we look at some of Shavu'ot's other themes, then it is possible to find some more straightforward associations with the plant world. The Torah emphasizes the festival's botanic and agricultural dimensions in connection with the wheat and barley harvests, and most notably as the beginning of the season for bringing the *bikkurim*, the first offerings of the summer fruit. With respect to the latter motif, the Mishnah declared that Shavu'ot is the "Rosh Hashanah," the annual day of judgment, for the fruit-trees.

Ultimately, this overabundance of explanations for the Shavu'ot greenery raised some serious doubts about whether *any* of them could be authentic. Some Jewish religious authorities began to suspect that there might be something un-

Jewish about the whole phenomenon. Particular discomfort was felt at the more ornate manifestations, which could involve festooning the ark, walls, and doors of the synagogue with actual trees and bushes.

A call to abolish the custom was voiced by Rabbi Elijah, the *Ga'on* of Vilna, and his cause was afterward taken up by several important Lithuanian Rabbis.

Now the *Ga'on* was rarely enthusiastic about any popular customs that were not firmly rooted in the literary sources of Jewish law. In the present instance, however, he had specific grounds for his objections: The practice of placing trees in the synagogue bore a disturbing resemblance to what went on in the churches on Christian holy days.

The *Hayei Adam*, a halakhic digest by Rabbi Abraham Danzig, associates the practice with the *Pfingsten*, the Christian Pentecost, which falls fifty days after Easter (around May 15) and parallels several themes from the Jewish Shavu'ot, such as revelation, baptism of converts, and all-night vigils. As frequently occurred, the churches had apparently also incorporated some pre-Christian nature rites into its religious ceremonies. The *Ga'on* and his followers thus saw the Jewish practice as a transparent violation of the biblical prohibition against adopting gentile ways, and prohibited the placing of trees in the sanctuaries.

The ban was accepted, with varying degrees of stringency, in many (but by no means all) Jewish communities.

Perhaps it was in order to compensate for the elimination of real trees and flowers from the holiday decorations that Ashkenazic Jews developed the lovely tradition of adorning the walls and windows with the intricate geometric papercuts that are referred to in Yiddish as *Reyzelakh* "little roses."

Though they are supposedly intended to evoke the symmetry of flowers, somehow, in our Alberta climate they tend to remind me more of snowflakes.

What Does the *Akdamut* Teach Us about Ashkenazic Origins?

During the late seventeenth century, the Jewish community in Venice was torn apart by a controversy. The issue that had the Venetian Jews raging at one another was a trivial-looking item of the Shavu'ot liturgy: When to recite the *Akdamut*?

The *Akdamut* is a rhymed poetic prologue to the festival Torah reading of the revelation at Mount Sinai. Composed by a cantor in Germany at the time of the Crusades, its ninety Aramaic stanzas speak in praise of the Torah and of the great rewards that await those who devote their lives to it.

Although the recitation of this inspiring poem had spread beyond the confines of the German and Polish rites, there emerged a slight discrepancy over where exactly it should be inserted. The established Ashkenazic custom was to chant it after the first reader, usually the *Kohen*, had read the first verse of his *aliyyah*.

The Sepharadic Jews of Venice were understandably perplexed by this strange practice. On no other occasion is it permissible to interrupt the sequence of the Torah reading for the sake of a prayer or liturgical poem, and there was no apparent justification for doing so now.

The Venetian Jews were so polarized on the issue that they eventually involved an outsider, Rabbi Ephraim Cohen of Vilna. In his *responsum* on the question, the Lithuanian sage came out solidly in favor of the Ashkenazic practice, appealing to its antiquity and to the sacred duty of following ancestral custom, even if it is not readily understandable.

Several of the elements in this controversy can be viewed as typical of the differing Ashkenazic and Sepharadic attitudes toward local custom.

The Sepharadim, representatives of a culture that esteemed rationalism and systematic thinking, insisted that practice must conform to the theoretical demands of the halakhah. Where conflicts arise it is the custom that must yield to the law.

By contrast, the Jews of central Europe had been distinguished from their earliest days by a profound reverence for their local customs. Lacking the Sepharadic inclination for systematic codification, early Ashkenazic Jewry channeled their literary energies to recording meticulously the customs of individual communities and rabbis. Where their customs seemed to conflict with the requirements of the Talmud, then it was the Talmud that had to be reinterpreted so as to uphold the customs.

It is likely that this veneration of ancestral ritual was inspired by the consciousness that their forebears had subjected themselves to heroic martyrdom at the sword of the Crusaders, the very same setting that had produced the *Akdamut*.

Through their unyielding adherence to custom, Ashkenazic Jewry succeeded in preserving vestiges of ancient traditions, even though the historical roots were unknown to them.

This is certainly true in the instance of the *Akdamut* controversy. Although the defenders of the Ashkenazic rite were usually at a loss to explain it, we are now able to trace its origins back to ancient synagogue procedure.

According to the procedures described in the Talmud, the reading of each verse from the Scriptures must be followed by the recitation of its Aramaic translation, known as a Targum. The purpose was to make the Hebrew text accessible to worshippers who were not well-versed in the holy tongue. With the decline of Aramaic as a Jewish vernacular the practice has fallen into disuse in most communities, but it remains on the books.

The recitation of the Targum would thus begin *after the reading of the first verse of the Torah reading*. With this fact in mind, it makes perfect sense that the *Akdamut*, which is composed in Aramaic, should be inserted at that point in the reading if it was actually the beginning of the Targum, and not of the Torah reading itself.

Although the *Akdamut* is *not* a translation of the opening verse of the Torah reading, but a poem in its own right, the phenomenon can still be accounted for by our knowledge of the history of the Targum literature.

The Targums that were employed in the Land of Israel were elaborate literary creations that wove together elements from midrash and traditional teaching. The *Turgeman*, the official responsible for reciting the Targum during the service, was expected to improvise his text. Indeed, this preference for creative improvisation over uniformity and standardization was another characteristic difference between the Palestinian and Babylonian liturgies.

As a natural extension to their artistic Targums, the *Turgeman*s of the Land of Israel were accustomed to composing dramatic introductory passages for "special" occasions. Several of these have survived in manuscripts.

Thus, in one text, the story of the parting of the Red Sea is introduced by a long alphabetical poem in which Moses debates with the sea over the Israelites' right to pass through. The sea refuses to relent until Moses appeals to divine authority. The same manuscript contains a prelude to the giving of the Torah, in which hosts of angels and supernatural beings celebrate the mystical wedding of God and his people.

Of course, the Shavu'ot reading of the Sinai revelation is a very special one and so the theme attracted a number of poetic creations.

Thus we can recognize that in fashioning this targumic prelude, the eleventh-century author of the *Akdamut* was continuing a tradition whose roots lay deep in the Holy Land. Removed from its original setting of a full Aramaic translation, the placement of the *Akdamut* seemed an incomprehensible deviation from normative practice.

This instance provides additional confirmation for a pattern that has often been discerned by historians of Ashkenazic Jewry: that the community originated in the Land of Israel, having reached Germany via Italy and France. This route can be traced through the strata of the Yiddish language as well as through many of their rituals and customs. Sepharadic Jews, on the other hand, can be linked to Babylonia.

Thanks to their fervent devotion to local customs, the Ashkenazic Jews of Venice and elsewhere have allowed us access to precious treasures from our past.

CALENDRICAL CURIOSITIES

What Does the Talmud
Say about January 1?

All Jews living in the Christian culture of western society must have felt the discomfort that comes with standing on the sidelines while our neighbors celebrate their holidays at this time of year. Most of us are diligent about respectfully disassociating ourselves from the obvious religious implications of Christmas.

The "civil" New Year, on the other hand, appears to be another matter altogether. This is a day that does not have any denominational message, a mere symbolic commemoration of the start of a new year in the calendar that we all use in our day-to-day lives.

When we look back to the talmudic sources we find that our ancient rabbis make explicit reference to New Years' Day whereas the celebration of Christmas was, as far as I know, quite unknown to them.

The passages in question speak of the Roman festival of the Kalends, that is, the *Kalendae Januariae* (etymologically related to our English word "calendar"), which celebrated the New Year in Roman times. The day is mentioned in the Mishnah (*Avodah Zarah* 1:3) in a list of various Roman festivities on which Jews are required to avoid doing business with the pagans so as not to add to the worshipper's pleasure or appear to be showing honor to their idols.

Though they were aware that these festivals were being observed throughout the Roman world, the talmudic
sages were not always clear about their purposes and origins. They offered some interesting suggestions about how
the Kalends came to be and why it was celebrated in the way
it was.

ADAM'S CELEBRATION

One assumption that the rabbis frequently held was that
pagan religion was somehow a corruption of authentic biblical traditions that had become misunderstood with the
passage of time. Accordingly the Talmud would look for
precedents for the respective holidays in the actions of the
ancestors of these nations, including figures such as Esau
(he was, according to rabbinic tradition, the progenitor of
the Romans) or Adam, the father of all mankind.

Following this premise, for example, the Talmud records
that the Egyptians' cult of Serapis had originated in their
veneration of Joseph. Another source relates how the Egyptians had come to worship the ibis birds because Moses had
used them in his military campaigns against the Ethiopians.
Many similar instances of this phenomenon could easily be
adduced.

A comparable approach was used by the prominent
third-century Babylonian teacher Rav to explain the origin
of the Roman New Year. According to Rav's account it was
Adam, the first man, who had instituted the Kalends.

Because in the very first year of his life he had no way
of knowing the cyclical seasonal changes that occur in the
lengths of the days, Adam became very disturbed when the
first winter began to approach and he saw that the days were
getting shorter and the nights longer. He began to fear that

the day was being consumed by a cosmic serpent, and that the pattern would persist indefinitely until daylight disappeared altogether.

This dread continued to trouble Adam until the arrival of the winter solstice, when the pattern began to reverse itself and the days began to lengthen. At this point, relates Rav, Adam—in an allusion to what would become known as the Kalends—exclaimed *Kalon dio*, a Greek phrase that has been construed by assorted modern scholars as meaning, "Praise be to God," "Beautiful day," or "May the sun set well."

From that day onward, the Talmud concludes, the day of the solstice has been observed by Adam's descendants, though the original reason may have been garbled in the transmission.

A MYTHOLOGICAL MOTIF

Another noted talmudic rabbi, Yohanan, proposed a different explanation of the origin of the Kalends. This version of the story has nothing to do with biblical history, but goes back to a heroic exploit in Roman history.

> Once, during a war between Rome and Egypt, the two sides, recognizing the futility of continued combat, decided to award the victory to whichever general would agree to sacrifice his life by falling on his sword.
>
> The Roman general, an old man named Januarius, was persuaded to pay the ultimate price when he was assured that his twelve sons would be honored with noble titles as dukes, hyparchs, and generals.

> After he had performed the heroic deed, they renamed the day, in his honor, "the Kalendes of Januarius."

It would appear that Rabbi Yohanan has interpreted the New Year Festival as a purely national holiday without any objectionable religious connotations. A closer look at the story, however, reveals some clearly mythological motifs.

For example, the twelve sons bear a suspicious resemblance to the twelve months of the year that are being renewed at this point in time.

The general Januarius reminds us of the two-faced Roman divinity Janus who is actually being honored on this day and who gives his name to the first month.

According to some scholars Janus was originally worshipped by the Etruscans as a god of Light and Day—a connection that fits in very nicely with Rav's legend of Adam and the shortening days. As a two-faced deity, Janus was believed to look simultaneously at the past and the future, and hence he was selected as the appropriate god for the new year.

Though a similar account of a King Janus is recorded in a later Christian source, that story certainly does not refer to an actual historical event. Some scholars have explained that underlying Rabbi Yohanan's account is an old myth about how the ancient god Janus, the father of Time, died to make room for his twelve sons, the twelve months.

Presupposed by all these talmudic explanations is the firm conviction that January 1 is not merely a Roman civil holiday, but a pagan religious celebration.

By participating in its festivities, Jews would show honor to idols and to their most hated enemy, the "Kingdom of Wickedness," Rome.

Is There a Jewish Mother's Day?

There is a sort of Mother's Day that is observed in Israel, especially among the pre-schoolers. This occasion, on which the toddlers are usually guided in making crafts for their mothers, is observed on the eleventh day of the Hebrew month of Heshvan (around October or November). It is a rather modest affair, lacking both the strict halakhic definition of a full-fledged religious holiday and the commercial hype of its American counterpart.

The choice of this date is an intriguing one. It falls on the traditional date of the death of the matriarch Rachel. I have not yet succeeded in tracing the derivation of this date, which is not mentioned in the Bible, talmudic literature, or any of the medieval writings that I have been able to consult. My guess is that its origins are to be found somewhere in the sixteenth-century, when the Spanish Expulsion brought many Jews to the soil of the Holy Land. The kabbalists had a special penchant for visiting the graves of the righteous, and evolved detailed calendars for pilgrimages to the burial sites of pious Jews of earlier times, including Rachel's tomb on the road to Bethlehem. The eleventh of Heshvan was likely selected as a date for such a pilgrimage. There are some older midrashic traditions to the effect that two other Hebrew matriarchs, Sarah and Rebecca, died around the same time of the year.

The transformation of Rachel's *yahrzeit* into a "Mother's Day" raises the question: What is there in Rachel's life and personality that makes her a suitable embodiment of the Jewish ideals of motherhood? Like many biblical heroines, Rachel did not have an easy time achieving motherhood, and for much of her married life had to resign herself to watching her sister Leah bear Jacob many children, until she herself finally gave birth to Joseph. Not long afterward she expired while giving birth to Benjamin. While she did not have much opportunity to enjoy the blessings of motherhood— or perhaps precisely for this reason—the prophet Jeremiah depicted her poetically as the archetypal mother of the nation. It was she who wept as her children were sent off into exile, and who would most rejoice at their return from captivity. In Jewish folklore and in the mystical tradition Rachel was identified with the Divine Presence (the *Shekhinah*), and came to be depicted as the spiritual mother of the entire Jewish people, following the fate of her children through their wanderings and remaining inconsolable until their reunification.

The commemoration of Rachel's *yahrzeit* came to be observed with particular intensity among Ashkenazic women. This can be seen in the tradition of *Tekhinnes*, the Yiddish prayers that constituted a vital part of women's day-to-day religious life, and often made reference to pious Jewish women of earlier ages. The *Tekhinneh* literature developed an elaborate set of prayers for Rosh Hodesh, the first days of each of the Jewish months (which had previously been observed as women's holidays). One of the popular *tekhinnes* for the month of Heshvan contains a touching appeal to Rachel, bidding her to strike on the heavenly Gates of Mercy in order to intercede before God to insure that he fulfil his pledge to her, to deliver her children from exile: Just as they passed by Rachel's grave on their way out of the Land of Israel, so will they now pass by on their return to their land.

The important themes that are embodied in the life of the historic Rachel, as well as in her stature as a national symbol, make her a worthy figure upon which to focus a Jewish Mother's Day.

Is Columbus Day a Jewish Holiday?

October 14 is commemorated by Americans as Columbus Day. Now this fact would not normally deserve mention in a Jewish book. As we shall see in a moment, however, there has been some weighty scholarly debate over the possibility that Columbus, though undeniably a devout and zealous Catholic, might also have been the proud descendant of Spanish Jews. Ironically, this view has been championed by some patriotic Spaniards, who would rather have him a Spanish Jew than an Italian gentile.

Here are a few of the interesting facts that have been raised in connection with this question:

- There is evidence that Columbus spoke Spanish while still living in Italy, an unusual situation unless his family had originated in Spain. Spanish-speaking Jewish refugees from the Inquisition were numerous in the Genoa area.
- The form "Colón" that Columbus adopted as the Spanish equivalent of his last name was not the expected form (which would have been "Colom" or "Colombo"). It was however a common Jewish variation on the name.

- Columbus was known to frequent the company of Jews and former Jews, among whom were some noted astronomers and navigators, as well as his official translator. Marranos figure prominently among Columbus' backers and crew. Throughout his life he demonstrated a keen knowledge of the Bible and the geography of the Holy Land. In fact, in one place he calculated the date from the destruction of the "Second House" [that is, Temple], counting from the traditional (and erroneous) Jewish date of 68 C.E., rather than the generally held 70 C.E.
- Columbus began the official report of his first voyage to America, addressed to Ferdinand and Isabella, with the following words: "And thus, having expelled all the Jews from all your kingdoms and dominions, in the month of January, Your Highnesses commanded me that . . . I should go to the said parts of India." This is a strange fact to mention in this context, and it is not even correct: The order of expulsion was not signed until March 31!
- The connections between the timing of Columbus's voyage and the expulsion of Spanish Jewry are indeed curious. Historians have noted that, though Columbus was not scheduled to set sail until August 3, he insisted that his entire crew be ready on board a full day earlier. The timing becomes more intriguing when we consider that August 2, 1492, was the day that had been ordained for the last Jews of Spain to depart the country. Hundreds of thousands of Jews were departing Spain on that black day.
- When this coincidence of dates was first noted by the Spanish biographer S. de Madariaga, the English Jewish historian Cecil Roth supplemented it with a

further "coincidence": August 2, 1492, coincided with the Ninth of Av, the Jewish fast of mourning for the destruction of the Jerusalem Temples! It was as if Columbus had arranged to remain on board ship for that ill-omened day, and to depart only afterward.

It would be impossible, in the context of a short article, to enumerate all the evidence that has been adduced on this question. De Madariaga devoted a five-hundred-page tome to proving this thesis. Some of the most important arguments are, however, summarized in the relevant entry in the *Encyclopedia Judaica*, written by the encyclopedia's editor-in-chief, Cecil Roth. While Roth himself expresses some skepticism about the explorer's Jewish origins, it is significant that the entry is not preceded by the special sign that normally indicates articles about non-Jews.

Perhaps Columbus Day is, after all, a Jewish holiday.

For Further Reading

Is Tsholent the Ultimate Jewish Food?
Stern, Menahem. *Greek and Latin Authors on Jews and Judaism.* Publications of the Israel Academy of Sciences, Section of Humanities. Jerusalem: The Israel Academy of Sciences and Humanities, 1974–1984.
Roth, Cecil. *A History of the Marranos.* Harper Torchbooks, The Temple Library. New York: Harper & Row, 1966.

Why Do We Light Two Candles on Shabbat?
Ta-Shma, Israel. "Ner Shel Kavod." *Tarbiz* 45 (1976): 128–137.

Why Do We Invite Angels to the Shabbat Table?
Jacobson, I. *Netiv Binah.* Tel-Aviv: Sinai, 1968.

ROSH HASHANAH

Why Is Rosh Hashanah Like a Courtroom Trial?
Goodman, Phillip. *The Rosh Hashanah Anthology.* Philadelphia: Jewish Publication Society of America, 1973.

Urbach, E. *The Sages: Their Concepts and Beliefs*. Translated by I. Abrahams. Cambridge, Mass. and London, England: Harvard University Press, 1987.

Where Are We Casting Those Sins?
Lauterbach, Jacob Z. "Tashlikh—A Study in Jewish Ceremonies." *Hebrew Union College Annual* 11 (1936): 207–340.

What Are the Origins of Synagogue Poetry?
Fleischer, Ezra. *Hebrew Liturgical Poetry in the Middle Ages*. Keter Library, Jewish People and Culture. Edited by S. Halkin. Jerusalem: Keter, 1975.
Rabinovitz, Zvi Meir, ed. *The Liturgical Poems of Rabbi Yannai According to the Triennial Cycle of the Pentateuch and the Holidays: Critical Edition with Introduction and Commentary*. Jerusalem: Mosad Bialik and Tel-Aviv University, 1985–1987.

How Did the Canadian Pioneers
Assemble a Minyan for the Holidays?
Chiel, Arthur A. *The Jews in Manitoba: a Social History*. Historical and Scientific Society of Manitoba, Toronto: University of Toronto Press, 1961.
Leonoff, Cyril Edel. *Pioneers, Pedlars, and Prayer Shawls: The Jewish Communities in British Columbia and the Yukon*. Victoria: Sono Nis Press, 1978.
Rosenberg, Stuart E. *The Jewish Community in Canada*. Vol. 2. Toronto and Montreal: McClelland and Stewart, 1971.

What Year Is It Today?
Frank, Edgar. *Talmudic and Rabbinical Chronology: The Systems of Counting Years in Jewish Literature*. New York: Feldheim, 1956.

Friedman, Mordechai Akiva. *Jewish Marriage in Palestine: A Cairo Geniza Study.* Tel-Aviv and New York: Tel-Aviv University and the Jewish Theological Seminary of America, 1980.

Lieberman, Saul. *Tosefta ki-fshutah.* Vol. 8. New York: The Jewish Theological Seminary of America, 1973.

Milikowsky, Chaim. "Seder Olam: A Rabbinic Chronology." Ph. D. diss., Yale University, 1981.

Roth, Cecil. *The Jews in the Renaissance.* Harper Torchbooks. Edited by Temple Library. New York: Harper & Row, 1959.

YOM KIPPUR

Is There an Islamic Yom Kippur?

Katsh, Abraham I. *Judaism in Islam, Biblical and Talmudic Backgrounds of the Koran and Its Commentaries: Suras II and III.* New York: Bloch for New York University Press, 1980.

Lazarus-Yafeh, Hava. *Some Religious Aspects of Islam: A Collection of Articles.* Leiden: Brill, 1981.

Why Has the Kol Nidré Been So Controversial?

Zevin, S. J. et al., ed. *Talmudic Encyclopedia.* Jerusalem: Talmudic Encyclopedia Institute, 1978–.

What Was Wrong with the Repentance of the Ninevites?

Urbach, E. E. "The Repentance of the People of Nineveh and the Discussions between Jews and Christians." *Tarbiz* 20 (1949): 118–122.

How Have People Been Transformed by Yom Kippur?

Almond, Philip C. *Rudolf Otto, an Introduction to His Philosophical Theology.* Studies in Religion, Chapel Hill: University of North Carolina Press, 1984.

Glatzer, Nahum N. *Franz Rosenzweig: His Life and Thought*. Second revised ed. New York: Schocken, 1951.

Otto, Rudolph. *The Idea of the Holy*. Translated by John W. Harvey. New York: Oxford University Press, 1957.

SUKKOT

How Did Hosanna Become an English Word?
Brown, Raymond E., ed. *The Gospel According to John (i–x)*. The Anchor Bible. Garden City, NY: Doubleday, 1966.

What Happens in the Hoshana Rabbah Moonlight?
Jacobson, I. *Netiv Binah*. Tel-Aviv: Sinai, 1968.
Trachtenberg, Joshua. *Jewish Magic and Superstition*. First Atheneum ed. New York: Temple Books, 1970.
Zevin, S. J. et al., ed. *Talmudic Encyclopedia*. Jerusalem: Talmudic Encyclopedia Institute, 1978–.

How Rowdy Can It Get on Simhat Torah?
Yaari, Abraham. *Toledot Hag Simhat Torah*. Jerusalem: Mossad Harav Kook, 1964.

HANUKKAH

How Did the Maccabees Become Christian Martyrs?
Bickerman, Elias. *The God of the Maccabees: Studies on the Meaning and Origin of the Maccabean Revolt*. Translated by Horst R. Moehring. Studies in Judaism in Late Antiquity. Leiden: Brill, 1979.

What Is Hellenism?
Bickerman, Elias. *The God of the Maccabees: Studies on the Meaning and Origin of the Maccabean Revolt*.

Translated by Horst R. Moehring. Studies in Judaism in Late Antiquity. Leiden: Brill, 1979.

Lieberman, Saul. *Hellenism in Jewish Palestine: Studies in the Literary Transmission, Beliefs and Manners of Palestine in the 1st Century* B.C.E.–*4th Century* C.E. New York: The Jewish Theological Seminary of America, 1962.

Why Is Hanukkah Considered a Women's Holiday?

Eisenstein, J. D., ed. *Ozar Midrashim: Bibliotheca Midraschica*. Reprint ed., [Israel]: 1969.

Goodspeed, Edgar J. *The Apocrypha: An American Translation*. New York: Vintage, 1959.

Jellinek, Adolph, ed. *Bet ha-Midrasch*. Reprint ed., Jerusalem: Wahrmann, 1967.

Was Judah a "Hammerhead"?

Zeitlin, Solomon and Sidney Saul Tedesche, ed. *The First Book of Maccabees*. Jewish Apocryphal Literature. New York: Harper & Brothers for Dropsie College, 1950.

What Became of the Maccabees' Menorah?

Barag, Dan. "The Menorah as a Messianic Symbol during the Late Roman and Byzantine Periods." Paper presented at the Ninth Congress of Jewish Studies, Jerusalem, 1986, 1982.

Sperber, Daniel. "An Early Meaning of the Word Shapud." *Revue des Etudes Juives* 124 (1965): 179–184.

Sperber, Daniel. "The History of the Menorah." *Journal of Jewish Studies* 16 (1965): 135–159.

What Is the Origin of Hanukkah-Gelt?

Goodman, Phillip. *The Hanukkah Anthology*. Philadelphia: Jewish Publication Society of America, 1976.

Kafih, Joseph. *Jewish Life in Sanâ.* Studies and Texts, Jerusalem: Kiryat-Sefer for the Ben-Zvi Institute, the Hebrew University, 1982.

Rivkind, I. *Jewish Money in Folkways, Cultural History and Folklore.* New York: American Academy for Jewish Research, 1959.

Where Is the Tomb of the Last Hasmonean?
Grintz, J. M. "Ha-ketovet miggiv'at ha-mivtar—perush histori." *Sinai* 75 (1974): 20–23.

Lieberman, Saul. "Notes on the Giv'at ha-Mivtar Inscription." *P'raqim: Yearbook of the Schocken Institute for Jewish Research* 2 (1969–1974): 335–373.

Rosenthal, E. S. "The Giv'at ha-Mivtar Inscription." *P'raqim: Yearbook of the Schocken Institute for Jewish Research* 2 (1969–1974): 335–373.

Why did the Menorah Offend the Magi?
Frye, Richard N. *The Heritage of Persia.* Second ed., History of Civilisation, London: Weidenfeld and Nicolson, 1965.

Gafni, Isaiah M. *The Jews in Babylonia in the Talmudic Era: A Social and Cultural History.* Monographs in Jewish History. Edited by A. Grossman et al. Jerusalem: Zalman Shazar Center, 1990.

Rosenthal, E. S. "For the Talmudic Dictionary—Talmudica Iranica." In *Irano-Judaica: Studies relating to Jewish Contacts with Persian Culture throughout the Ages*, ed. Shaul Shaked. 38–134. Jerusalem: Ben-Zvi Institute, 1982.

Yarshater, Ehsan, ed. *The Cambridge History of Iran.* Cambridge: Cambridge University Press, 1983.

WINTER

What Is the Proper Date to Pray for Rain?
  Lasker, A. and D. "The Strange Case of December 4."
  Conservative Judaism 38 (1985): 91–99.

FIFTEENTH OF SHEVAT

Who Is The Incredible Plant-Man?
  Ginzberg, Louis. *The Legends of the Jews*. Translated by
  H. Szold. Philadelphia: Jewish Publication Society
  of America, 1909–1939.
  Sperber, Daniel. "Varia Midrashica II." *Revue des Etudes
  Juives* 131 (1972): 160–171.

PURIM

How Did Purim Turn into a Carnival?
  Davidson, Israel. *Parody in Jewish Literature*. Texts and
  Studies. New York: Jewish Theological Seminary
  of America, 1907.
  Shmeruk, Chone. *Yiddish Biblical Plays: 1697–1750*.
  Jerusalem: Israel Academy of Sciences and Hu-
  manities, 1979.

Why Was There a War against Purim?
  Bickerman, Elias. *Studies in Jewish and Christian
  History*. Arbeiten zur Geschichte des antiken Ju-
  dentums und des Urchristentums. Leiden: Brill,
  1976.
  Meyer, Michael. *The Origins of the Modern Jew: Jewish Identity and European Culture in Germany
  1749–1824*. Detroit: Wayne State University Press,
  1967.

Mendes-Flohr, Paul and Jehuda Reinharz, ed. *The Jew in the Modern World: A Documentary History*. Second ed., New York and Oxford: Oxford University Press, 1955.

Pullan, B. *The Jews of Europe and the Inquisition of Venice, 1550–1670*. Totowa: Barnes & Noble, 1983.

Roth, Cecil. *The Jews in the Renaissance*. Harper Torchbooks edition, Temple Library. New York: Harper & Row, 1959.

Was Vashti a Feminist Heroine?

Gendler, M. "The Restoration of Vashti." In *The Jewish Woman: New Perspectives*, Edited by E. Koltun. 241–247. New York: Schocken, 1976.

Ginzberg, Louis. *The Legends of the Jews*. Translated by H. Szold. Philadelphia: Jewish Publication Society of America, 1909–1939.

Was Esther the First Marrano?

Lazarus-Yafeh, H. "Queen Esther—One of the Marranos?" *Tarbiz* 57 (1 1987): 12–14.

Roth, Cecil. *A History of the Marranos*. Harper Torchbooks edition, Temple Library. New York: Harper & Row, 1966.

Is the Purim Story an Astrological Myth?

Walfish, Barry Dov. *Esther in Medieval Garb: Jewish Interpretation of the Book of Esther in the Middle Ages*. State University of New York, Studies in Judaica: Hermeneutics, Mysticism, and Religion. Edited by Michael Fishbane, Robert Goldenberg, and Arthur Green. Albany: State University of New York Press, 1993.

NISAN

What Is Special about the Month of Nisan?
Lichtenstein, Hans. "Die Fastenrölle, Eine Untersuchung zur jüdisch-hellenistischen Geschichte." *Hebrew Union College Annual* 8–9 (1931–1932): 257–351.
Yadin, Yigael, ed. *The Temple Scroll*. Jerusalem: Israel Exploration Society, 1983.

PASSOVER

Why Is the Seder Like a Roman Banquet?
Goodman, Phillip. *The Passover Anthology*. Philadelphia: Jewish Publication Society of America, 1961.
Stein, S. "The Influence of the Symposia Literature on the Literary Form of the Pesah Haggadah." *Journal of Jewish Studies* 7 (1957): 13–44.

What Is the Spiritual Symbolism of the Exodus?
Glatzer, Nahum N., ed. *The Essential Philo*. New York: Schocken, 1971.
Newman, Louis I. and Samuel Spitz, ed. *The Hasidic Anthology: Tales and Teachings of the Hasidim*. New York: Schocken, 1972.

What Is the Significance of the Had Gadya?
Fox, Harry. "On the History of the Songs 'Ehad Mi Yodea' and 'Had Gadya' among Jews and Gentiles." *Asufot* (2 1988): 111–126.
Kasher, M. M. *Hagadah Shelema, the Complete Pasover Hagada*. Jerusalem: Torah Shelema Institute, 1967.

Why Does Elijah Visit the Seder?
Ellinson, Eliakim G. *Ha-ishah Veha-mitzvot: Bein Ha-ishah Leyotzrah*. Jerusalem: World Zionist Move-

ment: Department of Jewish Religious Education in the Diaspora, 1984.

Kasher, M. M. *Hagadah Shelema, the Complete Pasover Hagada*. Jerusalem: Torah Shelema Institute, 1967.

Why Did American Jews Drink Raisin-Wine on Passover?

Sarna, Jonathan. "Passover Raisin Wine, The American Temperance Movement, and Mordecai Noah: The Origins, Meaning, and Wider Significance of a Nineteenth-Century American Jewish Religious Practice." *Hebrew Union College Annual* 59 (1988): 269–288.

Yahalom, S. "Jewish Existence in the Shadow of American Legislation: A Study of Prohibition." *Tarbiz* 53 (1983): 117–136.

Who is an "Important" Woman?

Ellinson, Eliakim G. *Ha-ishah Veha-mitzvot: Bein Ha-ishah Leyotzrah*. Jerusalem: World Zionist Movement: Department of Jewish Religious Education in the Diaspora, 1984.

Kasher, M. M. *Hagadah Shelema, the Complete Passover Hagada*. Jerusalem: Torah Shelema Institute, 1967.

Why Did Some Jews Dread Passover?

Handler, Andrew. *Blood Libel at Tiszaeszlar*. Boulder: East European Monographs, 1980.

Lieberman, Saul. *Tosefta ki-fshutah*. New York: The Jewish Theological Seminary of America, 1973.

Strack, Hermann L. *The Jews and Human Sacrifice: Human Blood and Jewish Ritual, an Historical and Sociological Inquiry*. Translated by Henry Blamchamp. 1909.

Trachtenberg, Joshua. *The Devil and the Jews: The Medieval Conception of the Jew and Its Relation to*

Modern Antisemitism. Reprint. Cleveland: World Publishing Company, 1961.

Who Staged the First Biblical Epic?
Gutman, Yehoshua. *The Beginnings of Jewish-Hellenistic Literature*. Jerusalem: Bialik Institute, 1969.
Jacobson, Howard. *The Exagogé of Ezekiel*. Cambridge: Cambridge University Press, 1983.

Why is the Reed Sea Red?
Avigad, Nahman and Yigael Yadin, ed. *A Genesis Apocryphon*. Jerusalem: Magnes Press and Heikhal Ha-Sefer, 1956.
Copisarow, M. "The Ancient Egyptian, Greek and Hebrew Concept of the Red Sea." *Vetus Testamentum* 12 (1962): 1–13.
Fitzmyer, Joseph A. *The Genesis Apocryphon of Qumran Cave 1: A Commentary*. Second ed., Biblica et Orientalia, Rome: Biblical Institute Press, 1971.

THE *OMER* SEASON

Why Was Judaism Split over the Counting of the Omer?
Grintz, J. "'Anshei Ha-Yahad,' Ha-isiyyim—Beit (E)Sin." *Sinai* 32 (1953): 37–46.
Talmon, Shemaryahu. "The Calendar Reckoning of the Sect from the Judean Desert." *Scripta Hierosolymitana* 4 (1958): 162–199.
Yadin, Yigael, ed. *The Temple Scroll*. Jerusalem: Israel Exploration Society, 1983.

Why Do We Mourn during the Omer Season?
Sperber, Daniel. *Minhagei yisra'el*. Jerusalem: Mossad Harav Kook, 1990–1991.

JERUSALEM REUNIFICATION DAY

Can a Palestinian Folktale Become a Midrash?
Scheiber, Sandor. "La Légende de l'emplacement du Temple de Jérusalem." In *Essays on Jewish Folklore and Comparative Literature*, ed. Alexander Scheiber. 64–69. Budapest: Akadémiai Kiadó, 1985.

SHAVU'OT

Who Was Obadiah the Proselyte?
Golb, Norman. "Megillat ovadiah ha-Ger," In *Studies in Geniza and Sepharadi Heritage Presented to Shelomo Dov Goitein*. Edited by Shelomo Morag and Issachar Ben-Ami. 77–107. Jerusalem: Magnes, 1981.

What Was the Shavu'ot Divorce Controversy?
Zevin, Shelomoh Yosef. *The Festivals in Halachah : An Analysis of the Development of the Festival Laws [ha-Mo'adim ba-halakah]*. Translated by Uri Kaploun and Meir Holder. New York and Jerusalem: ArtScroll Judaica Classics, 1982.

Why Do We Decorate the Synagogue with Greenery on Shavu'ot?
Sperber, Daniel. *Minhagei yisra'el*. Jerusalem: Mossad Harav Kook, 1990–1991.
Jacobson, I. *Netiv Binah*. Tel-Aviv: Sinai, 1968.

What Does the Akdamut *Teach Us about Ashkenazic Origins?*
Grossman, A. *The Early Sages of Ashkenaz*. Jerusalem: Magnes, 1981.
Heinemann, Joseph. "Remnants from the Poetic Creation of the Ancient Meturgemans." *Ha-Sifrut* 4 (1973): 362–375.

Jacobson, I. *Netiv Binah*. Tel-Aviv: Sinai, 1968.

Kasher, Rimon. "Two Targum-Tosephtas on the Death of Moses." *Tarbiz* 54 (1985): 217–224.

Zevin, Shelomoh Yosef. *The Festivals in Halachah : An Analysis of the Development of the Festival Laws [ha-Mo'adim ba-halakah]*. Translated by Uri Kaploun and Meir Holder. New York and Jerusalem: ArtScroll Judaica Classics, 1982.

CALENDRICAL CURIOSITIES

What Does the Talmud Say about January 1?

Lieberman, Saul. *Hellenism in Jewish Palestine: Studies in the Literary Transmission, Beliefs and Manners of Palestine in the 1st Century B.C.E.–4th Century C.E.* New York: The Jewish Theological Seminary of America, 1962.

Is There a Jewish Mother's Day?

Vilnay, Zev. *Legends of Judea and Samaria: Bethlehem, Hebron, Jericho, Dead Sea, Jaffa, Tel Aviv, Beersheba, Shechem, Sharon, Caesarea*. The Sacred Land. Edited by Zev Vilnay. 1st ed. Philadelphia: Jewish Publication Society of America, 1975.

Weissler, Chava. *Voices of the Matriarchs: Listening to the Prayers of Early Modern Jewish Women*. Boston, Mass: Beacon Press, 1998.

Is Columbus Day a Jewish Holiday?

Madariaga, Salvador de. *Christopher Columbus, Being the Life of the Very Magnificent Lord Don Cristoból Colón*. 1939.

Roth, Cecil. "Who Was Columbus?" In *Personalities and Events in Jewish History*, 192–211. Philadelphia: Jewish Publication Society of America, 1953.

Original Publication

Each chapter in this collection is listed according to its original title, followed by the newspaper issue where it first appeared.

Is Tsholent the Ultimate Jewish Food?
Tsholent. *Jewish Free Press*, 20 January 1994, p. 9.

Why Do We Light Two Candles on Shabbat?
Shabbat Candles: To See or Not to See? *Jewish Free Press*, 2 November 1995, p. 8.

Why Do We Invite Angels to the Shabbat Table?
Angels on My Shoulder. *Jewish Free Press*, 8 February 1996, p. 8

Why Is Rosh Hashanah Like a Courtroom Trial?
The Day of Judgement. *Jewish Star*, November 1989, pp. 4, 18.

Where Are We Casting Those Sins?
Into the Depths of the Sea: Tashlikh in Jewish Law and Lore. *Jewish Free Press*, 15 September 1993, p. 18.

What Are the Origins of Synagogue Poetry?
Piyyut: The Poetry of Worship. *Jewish Free Press*, 8 September 1994, pp. 18–19.

How Did the Canadian Pioneers Assemble a Minyan for the Holidays?
A *Minyan* for the Holidays. *Jewish Free Press*, 12 September 1996, p. 18.

What Year Is It Today?
What Year Is It Today? *Jewish Free Press*, 2 October 1997, pp. 20–21.

Is There an Islamic Yom Kippur?
The Islamic Yom Kippur. *Jewish Star*, Calgary, 9 September 1988, p. 4; Edmonton, 6 October 1988, p. 8.

Why Has the Kol Nidré Been So Controversial?
The Kol Nidre Controversy. *Jewish Free Press*, 6 September 1991, p. 7.

What Was Wrong with the Repentance of the Ninevites?
The Repentance of Nineveh. *Jewish Free Press*, 21 September 1995, p. 18.

How Have People Been Transformed by Yom Kippur?
Yom Kippur: Encounters with the Absolute. *The Calgary Herald*, 23 September 1996, p. A6, as "Yom Kippur Bridges Gap to God."

How Did *Hosanna* Become an English Word?
Hosanna. *Jewish Free Press*, 29 September 1993, pp. 10–11.

What Happens in the Hoshana Rabbah Moonlight?
I'm Bein' Followed by a Moonshadow . . . . *Jewish Free Press*, 5 October 1995, p. 8.

How Rowdy Can It Get on Simhat Torah?
Simhat Torah: The Rabbis and the Rabble. *Jewish Free Press*, 26 September 1996, p. 6.

How Did the Maccabees Become Christian Martyrs?
The "Holy Maccabee Martyrs." *Jewish Star*, 2–15 December 1988, pp. 4, 15.

What Is the Spiritual Aura of Hanukkah?
By the Hanukkah Lights. *Jewish Free Press*, 30 November 1990, p. 16.

What Is Hellenism?
Hellenism Revisited. *Jewish Free Press*, 15 November 1991, p. 15.

Why Is Hanukkah Considered a Women's Holiday?
"Because They Were Included in the Miracle." *Jewish Free Press*, 9 December 1993, pp. 11, 13.

Was Judah a "Hammerhead"?
Heroes, Hammers, and Hanukkah. *Jewish Free Press*, 30 November 1994, p. 10.

What Became of the Maccabees' Menorah?
The Maccabees' Menorah and Titus' Menorah. *Jewish Free Press*, 15 December 1996, pp. 14, 17.

What Is the Origin of *Hanukkah-Gelt?*
From Gelt to Gifts. *Jewish Free Press*, 21 November 1996, p. 12.

Where Is the Tomb of the Last Hasmonean?
The Tomb of the Last Hasmonean? *Jewish Free Press*, 5 December 1996, p. 16.

Why Did the Menorah Offend the Magi?
The Menorah and the Magi. *Jewish Free Press*, 19 December 1997, p. 18.

What Is the Proper Date to Pray for Rain?
Calendar Conundrums. *Jewish Free Press*, 15 December 1995, p. 7.

Who Is the Incredible Plant-Man?
  The Incredible Plant-Man. *Jewish Free Press*, 3 February 1994, p. 10.

How Did Purim Turn into a Carnival?
  Purim, Parody and Pilpul. *Jewish Star*, Calgary, 19 February 1988, p. 7; Edmonton, 10 March 1988, p. 9.

Why Was There a War against Purim?
  The War Against Purim. *Jewish Star*, Edmonton, March 1989, pp. 4–5.

Was Vashti a Feminist Heroine?
  Vashti: A Feminist Heroine? *Jewish Free Press*, 1 March 1991, p. 8.

Was Esther the First Marrano?
  Esther the Marrano. *Jewish Free Press*, 2 March 1995.

Is the Purim Story an Astrological Myth?
  Aquarian Esther. *Jewish Free Press*, 20 March 1997, pp. 8, 11.

What Is Special about the Month of Nisan?
  Nisan: the First Month. *Jewish Free Press*, 31 March 1992, p. 8.

Why Is the Seder Like a Roman Banquet?
  The Seder as a Living Tradition. *Jewish Star*, Calgary, 11 March 1988; Edmonton, 31 March 1988.

What Is the Spiritual Symbolism of the Exodus?
  The Exodus of the Spirit. *Jewish Star*, 6 April 1990, pp. 4, 14.

How Does Passover Celebrate Freedom?
  It Is the Season of Our Liberation. *Calgary Herald*, 23 March 1991, p. B11.

What Is the Significance of the Had Gadya?
That Remarkable Kid. *Jewish Free Press*, 15 April 1992,
p. 13.

Why Does Elijah Visit the Seder?
The Invisible Guest. *Jewish Free Press*, 30 March 1994,
p. 19.

Why Did American Jews Drink Raisin-Wine on Passover?
The Great Passover Raisin-Wine Controversy. *Jewish
Free Press*, 13 April 1995, p. 17.

Who is an "Important" Woman?
Important Women. *Jewish Free Press*, 4 April 1996, p. 16.

Why Did Some Jews Dread Passover?
A Text Inscribed in Blood. *Jewish Free Press*, 7 March
1996.

Who Staged the First Biblical Epic?
Staging the Exodus. *Jewish Free Press*, 21 April 1997,
pp. 18–19.

Why is the Reed Sea Red?
Red Sea, Reed Sea . . . and the Persian Gulf. *Jewish Free
Press*, 29 March 1991, p. 11.

Why Was Judaism Split over the Counting of the Omer?
New Light on an Ancient Ritual. *Jewish Star*, 31 March
1988, pp. 8–9.

Why Do We Mourn during the Omer Season?
The Tragic History of the "Omer" Season. *Jewish Free
Press*, 18 May 1995, p. 8.

Were There Really Two Thousand Years of Exile?
Two Thousand Years. *Jewish Free Press*, 4 May 1995,
p. 9.

Can a Palestinian Folktale Become a Midrash?
The Founding of Jerusalem: A Palestinian Midrash?
Jewish Free Press, 5 May 1994, pp. 8–9.

Who Was Obadiah the Proselyte?
Obadiah the Proselyte. *Jewish Free Press*, 17 June 1992,
p. 9.

What Was the Shavu'ot Divorce Controversy?
Tradition or Compassion: A Shavu'ot Controversy. *Jewish Free Press*, 1 June 1995, pp. 6–7.

Why Do We Decorate the Synagogue with
Greenery on *Shavu'ot*?
The Greening of Shavu'ot. *Jewish Free Press*, 23 May
1996, p. 7.

What Does the *Akdamut* Teach Us about
Ashkenazic Origins?
Akdamut, Aramaic, and Ashkenazic Origins. *Jewish Free Press*, 12 June 1997, p. 6.

What Does the Talmud Say about January 1?
January 1. *Jewish Star*, 22 December 1989, pp. 4, 19.

Is There a Jewish Mother's Day?
On Matriarch Rachel and Mother's Day. *Jewish Free Press*, 1 May 1991, p. 7.

Is Columbus Day a Jewish Holiday?
Columbus' Medinah? *Jewish Free Press*, 14 October
1991, p. 9.

Index

Abraham, 174
Abudraham, Rabbi David,
    59–60
Adam, 73, 222–224
adnei hasadeh, 107–111
Aeschylus, 172
afikoman, 87, 145–146
Africa, significance in
    Exodus, 170–172
agricultural significance of
    holidays, 58–60, 184
agunah, 209
Ahashverosh, King, 116,
    124–126, 131–133
Ahriman, Magi god of evil, 96
Akdamut, 215–218
Akiva, Rabbi, 185
Al-Bukhari, 38
alcohol
    consumed on Purim,
        115–119
    Passover, fifth cup of
        wine for, 157–158

Alexander the Great, 75
al-Madinah community,
    37
Amidah festival, 24
Andreas of Bari, 206
angels, Sabbath and, 9–11
annulment of vows,
    42–44
Antigonus, 90–93
Antiochos Epiphanes, 69,
    70, 72, 74
*Antisemitische
    Corrospondenz*
    (Rohling), 167–168
anti-Semitism
    Maccabees and, 70
    Passover and, 166–168
    Purim and, 121–123
    Temperance Movement
        and, 161
Antony, Marc, 91
Apocrypha, 68–69
apologists, Christian, 47

Aramaic language, 37
   Had Gadya recitation,
      154
   Hosanna, meaning of,
      55–56
   Samaritan inscription,
      91
   Targum, 217
Arch of Titus, 84
Aristobulus II, 90–92
Ashkenazim, 25, 31–32
   food, 3–5
   Had Gadya, 153
   Hoshana Rabbah, 60
   La'g Ba'omer, 186
   origin of, 218
   Passover wine, 158
   Sabbath candles, 6–7
   Shavu'ot, 214
   Tekhinnes prayers, 226–
      227
Ashura fast, 38, 40
astrology, 131–133
atonement. *see* Yom Kippur
attorneys, court
   prohibitions against,
      16
Auschwitz, 19
Autumnal Equinox, 101–
      103
Averroës. *see* Ibn Rushd
Av Harahamim prayer, 186
Azulai, Rabbi Hayyim
   Joseph David, 155

Ba'al Shem Tov, Rabbi
   Israel, 88
Babylonia, 194
   Kol Nidré, 43
   Magi, 94–97
   Passover wine tradition
      in, 158
   rabbinate, 25
   rain, praying for, 101,
      102
   Sephardic origin, 218
Babylonian Talmud, 17, 20,
      29–30, 185. *see also*
      Talmud
   on *Habbars,* 94
   Ninevites, repentance of,
      45
   Purim, 116
   on seder, 146
Baghdadi Caliphate, 31
"BaH," 71
baian (palm fronds), 17
Baitusim, 181–183
banning of books, 32
Bar Kokhba revolt, 185,
      195
"Bavli," 116
"Bayit Hadash" (Sirkes),
      71–72
beit sin (house of Sin), 182–
      183
ben Asher, Rabbi Bahya,
      59, 132
ben Chorin, Schalom, 123

ben Halafta, Rabbi Yosé, 30–31
ben Kalonymus, Rabbi Meir, 108
ben Levi, Rabbi Joshua, 77
ben Meir, Rabbi Samuel, 78, 164
ben Nahman, Rabbi Moses, 59
Bible, 129
    Alexandrian Jewish Bible, 68
    New Testament, 56
    Purim, inclusion of, 121
bikkurim (summer fruit), 213
Blackman, Abraham, 27
"Blood Accusations," 167–168
Book of Daniel, 32
Book of Esther, 120
Book of Jonah, 45–47
Book of Jubilees, 138, 182
Book of Judges, 79
Book of Judith, 79
Book of Ruth, 205
Books of Maccabees, 67–70, 78, 80. *see also* Maccabees
"box of hay," 5
British Columbia, 26–28
brothers, tale of two, 199–201
Buber, Martin, 50

burial, proper, 91–92
burning bush revelation, 171

calendrical calculations. *see* Hebrew calendar
Calgary, Canada, 27
Canada, Jewish pioneers in, 26–28
candles
    Hanukkah, 77
    Magi and, 94–97
    Sabbath, 6–8
Catholicism
    Holy Maccabees and, 69–70
    Julian calendar, 102
    Purim and, 121–122
    "Vulgate" text of Bible, 129
Chasam Sofer, 210
cheese, during Hanukkah, 78–79
children, custody of, 166
cholent. *see* tsholent
Christianity. *see also* conversion
    "barnacle goose," 109
    Book of Jonah and, 46–47
    dating of Jewish exile, 194
    Evangelical, 160–161
    Exodus and, 149–150
    Inquisition, 4–5, 127–130

Christianity (*continued*)
  intermediaries and, 10
  Maccabees as martyrs,
    67–70
  Palm Sunday, 56–57
  Pentecost, 214
  Purim and, 120–123
  Roman Empire and, 193
  Yom Kippur and, 48–49
Church and State,
  separation of, 161–162
Cohen, Rabbi Ephraim,
  215–216
coinage
  of Maccabees, 92
  symbols on, 83–86
Columbus, Christopher,
  228–230
commandment, concept of,
  43
commercialization of
  Hanukkah, 87–89
Commonwealth, Second,
  137
Conservative Judaism,
  Temperance Movement
  and, 161–162
conversion, 49–51, 127
  Friedlander and, 123
  Obadiah the Proselyte,
    205–207
  during Spanish
    Inquisition, 4–5,
    127–130

cooking on Sabbath, 3–5
Costa, Rabbi Israel, 200
creation, calculating date
  of, 29–33
Crusades, 70, 187, 206
crypto-Judaism, 127–130
custody of children, 166
Cyrene, 170

Daniel, Book of, 32
Danzig, Rabbi Abraham,
  214
dating systems, 29–33, 191–
  193. *see also* Hebrew
  calendar
David, King, 205
Dawson City, Canada, 27
Day of Atonement. *see* Yom
  Kippur
Day of Judgment, Rosh
  Hashanah as, 15–19
Dead Sea Scrolls, 137, 174,
  182–183
de Lamartine, Alphonse,
  200
Delitsch, Franz, 168
de Madariaga, S., 229–230
Demetrius, 170
de Rossi, Rabbi Azariah,
  32
Deuteronomy, 7
Diamond, Jacob, 27–28
Didymus lamp, 85
Dinah, 78

din Torah (lawsuit), 18–19
"documentary reckoning," 30

eagles, symbolism of, 85
"Edicts of Faith," 4–5. *see also* Spanish Inquisition
Efrem the Syrian, 47
Egypt, ancient, 68. *see also* Exodus; Passover
  Biblical interpretations in, 222
  as birthplace of wisdom, 170
  January 1 myth, 223–224
Eilat, Gulf of, 174
Elijah, 88, 156–158
Elijah, Rabbi, 214
El Orekh Din, 17
Emden, Rabbi, 10
Encyclopedia Judaica (Roth), 230
enemy, humanity of, 152
Enlightenment movement, 210
Epicurus, 75
Epstein, Rabbi Barukh, 60
equality among Jews, 138
Esau, 222
Essenes, 183
Esther, Queen, 77
  astrological interpretation of Purim, 131–133
  Book of, 120
  Christian views on, 121
  as Marrano, 127–130
  Purim story, origin of, 115–119
Esther Rabbah, 116
Etruscans, 224
etymology
  of *afikoman*, 145–146
  of calendar, 221
  of *Had Gadya*, 154
  Hanukkah *vs. hinnukh*, 87
  of Hasmonean names, 92
  of *Hosanna*, 55–57
  of Islamic terms, 37
  of Jewish settlement names, 194
  of Maccabee, 80–82
  of Obadiah the Proselyte, 206
  of *parpisa*, 21
  of tsholent, 4
European Jewry. *see* anti-Semitism; Ashkenazim; *individual nationalities*
evil, good *vs.*, 9
Exodus, 147–150. *see also* Passover
  dramatization of story, 169–172
  Sabbath, remembering, 7
  Shavu'ot greenery, 212
Exogogé (Ezekiel), 169–172
Ezekiel, 48

Ezekiel the Tragedian, 169–
   172
Ezra, 192

Fastnacht, 117
Fast of Esther, 128–129
Fast of Ramadan, 37–41
feminism, 124–126. *see also*
   women, roles in
   Judaism
Ferdinand, King, 229
festival, Sabbath as, 181
Festival of Lights. *see*
   Hanukkah
Festival of Weeks. *see*
   Shavu'ot
fire. *see also* candles
   offended Magi, 94–97
   Sabbath, prohibitions
      regarding, 62–63
First Hebrew Benevolent
   Society, 26–27
First Temple, 83. *see also*
   Second Temple
   destruction of, 116
   Omer season observance,
      179–180
   rebuilding of, 125
   site of, 199–201
fish, in *Tashlikh* ceremony,
   21
food, Jewish traditional
   cheese during Hanukkah,
      78–79

hamantaschen, 118–119
Haroset, 145
tsholent, 3–5
freedom, Passover
   celebration of, 151–152
French language, as source
   of Hebrew expressions,
   4
Friedlaender, David, 122–123

Gabriel, 126
Ga'on. see Ge'onim
Geiger, Abraham, 123
gelt, Hanukkah, 87–89
Genesis Apocryphon, 174
Genizah, 23, 205
geographic considerations
   for candle lighting, 7–8
Ge'onim, 20, 31, 185, 214
   Magi, writings about, 95–
      96
   on Simhat Torah, 61–63
German Jewry, 186
   Enlightenment
      movement, 210
   Purim and, 118, 122
get (divorce), 209
Ginzberg, Louis, 111, 126
God
   burning bush, 171
   El Orekh Din hymn, 17
   Exodus, 152
   judgment on Rosh
      Hashanah, 16–19

Golden Calf, 16
Gombiner, Rabbi Abraham, 63
good *vs.* evil, 9
Gospels, 46
Greece, ancient. *see also* Hellenism
   ancient culture of, 74–76, 78
   calendrical calculations of, 29–30
   mythology, 171–172
   names of Hasmoneans, 92
   seder and, 145
Greek language, 23, 74–76
Greek version of Torah. *see* Septuagint
greenery for Shavu'ot, 212–214
Gregorian calendar, 102
Gulf of Eilat, 174

Habbars, 94–96
Had Gadya, 153–155
Hadith (Muslim oral tradition), 38
Haggadah, 143, 148, 153–154
halakhic considerations
   of candles, 7
   of drunkenness on Purim, 117
   of Hoshana Rabbah, 60
   of Marranism, 128
   of Sabbath prayers, 10
halitzah ceremony, 209
Hallel prayer, 56, 57, 152
Haman, 72
   astrological interpretation of Purim, 131–133
   Christian views on, 120–121
   Purim story, origin of, 115–119
hamantaschen, 118–119
hametz, alcohol prohibition and, 159
Handel, G.F., 70
Hanukkah
   gelt, 87–89
   Hellenism and, 74–76
   Maccabees, 67–70
   Sabbath candles compared to, 7
   spiritual aura of, 71–73
   as women's holiday, 77–79
haroset, 145
Hart, Solomon, 28
Hasidism, 62
Hasmoneans, 74
   decline of, 90–93, 192
   Mattathias Antigonos, 83
Hatikvah (Israeli national anthem), 191–192, 195
Hayei Adam (Danzig), 214

Hayyim of Volzhim, 10–11
Hebrew Bible. *see* Bible
Hebrew calendar, 29–33
  Fast of Esther, 128
  Islamic interpretation of,
    39
  January 1, 221–224
  Nisan, 137–139
  observing holidays on
    second day, 208
  Omer season, calculating,
    180–184
  rain, praying for, 101–
    103
Hebrew language, 37, 80–
    81
Hellenism, 23, 74–76. *see
    also* Greece
  dramatizations of
    Exodus, 169–172
  judicial system, analogies
    to, 16
Hemdat Yamim, 87–88
Hercules, 170–171
Herod, King, 85, 90
Herodotus, 173
Hertz Imber, Naftali, 191
"Hida," 155
holiness in religion, 48–49
Holocaust, commemorating
    the, 187
Holosfernes, 79
Homer, 75
hosanna, 55–57

Hoshana Rabbah, 58–60
house of Sin, 182–183
humanity of enemy
    concept, 152
Hussein, Saddam, 125, 126

Ibn Daud, Rabbi Abraham,
    31
Ibn Ezra, Rabbi Abraham,
    127, 132
Ibn Rushd, 133
Idea of the Holy, The (Otto),
    49
importance, concept of,
    163–165
Inquisition, Christian, 4–5,
    127–130
Iraq, 102, 175. *see also*
    Babylonia
Isabella, Queen, 229
Isaiah, 48, 125
Islam
  Bait al-muqdasah, 199–
    201
  Mu'ahadin, 127
  Muslim Caliphate, 194
  similarities to Judaism,
    37–41
Israel, independence of,
    191–195
Isserles, Rabbi Moses, 60,
    212
Italian carnivals, influence
    on Purim, 117, 121–122

Italy, Christopher
Columbus and, 228
I'tikaf (last ten days of
Ramadan), 40

Jael, 79
Januarius, 223–224
Janus, King, 224
Jeremiah, 226
Jerome, Father, 46
Jerusalem
Givat Hamivtar
archaelogical site,
91–93
Hanukkah tradition in,
89
reunification, 199–201
Jerusalem Talmud, 77
Jerusalem Temple. *see* First
Temple; Second
Temple
Jesus, 56–57
dating of Jewish exile
and, 194
Haman as antithesis of,
121
Jonah, comparison to, 46
Last Supper, 160
Johanan the Hasmonean,
78
Johannes, 205–207
Jonah, Book of, 45–47
Joseph, 222
Joseph, Rabbi Jacob, 88

Josephus Flavius, 174
Jubilees, Book of, 138
Judah the Maccabee, 80–
82. *see also* Maccabees
"Judas Maccabeus," 70
Judges, Book of, 79
Judith, 78–79
Julian calendar, 102–103
Juvenal, 5

Kabbalah. *see also*
superstition
"Hida," 155
Hoshana Rabbah, 58–60
Rachel, *yahrzeit* of, 225–
227
Simhat Torah, influence
on, 63
Zohar, 149
Kaddish prayer, 19
Kalendae Januariae, 221
Kalen dio, 223
kapparot rite, 20–21
Karo, Rabbi Joseph, 32. *see
also Shulhan 'Arukh*
(Karo)
Kartir, 96–97
kategoros (defending
attorney), 16–19
Kedushah prayer, 48
Kedushta (poem), 24
Keturah, 170
Kila'im, 107–111
Klondike Gold Rush, 27

Kluger, Rabbi Solomon, 209
Kol Nidré, 42–44
Koran, 38, 40
Kurdish Jewish tradition for *Tashlikh* ceremony, 21

La'g ba'omer, mourning practices on, 185–186
Landau, Rabbi Eleazar, 209–211
Last Supper, 160
Latin language and Hebrew expressions, 21
law
    Rosh Hashanah compared to, 15–19
    value of, 47
leaning during seder, 143–146
Legends of the Jews, The (Ginzberg), 126
Levi, 78–79
Leviticus, 183–184
Libya, 170
Lifschutz, Rabbi Israel, 109–110
light, significance during Hanukkah, 71–73. *see also* candles; fire
liturgical poems. *see* poetry
Logos concept, 171–172
"lots" of Purim, 131–133

lulavim, 17, 55–56
Luther, Martin, 121

Ma'aleh Adumim, 183
Ma'aseh Nissim (Costa), 200
Maccabees, 192
    Books of, 78
    as Christian martyrs, 67–70
    as Hellenists, 75–76
Magi, 94–97
"Maharil," 212
Mahzor (cycle), 23–25
Maimonides, 43, 72, 127
    on plant-man, 109
    on Purim, 117
Manoah of Narbonne, 164
Ma'or Einayim (de Rossi), 32
Ma'oz Tzur song, 70
Marranos, 127–130
    Christopher Columbus as, 228–230
    raisin-wine and, 160
marriage, levirate, 209
Mattathias, 80
Mecca, prayers toward, 40
Megillah, 115
    Marrano interpretation, 129–130
    resistance to Purim, 120
Megillat Ta'anit, 138
Mendelssohn, Moses, 122

Menorah
  of the Maccabees, 83–86
  Magi and, 94–97
Messiah
  Christian views on, 56
  Elijah and advent of, 158
  expectations of, 103, 206
  Had Gadya commentary
    and, 154
  metaphor, used on Rosh
    Hashanah, 15–19
met mitzvah (burial), 92
Midian, 170–172
Midrash
  on Adam, 73
  Greek references in, 74–
    76
  on Jonah, 46
  on Purim, 131
Mikhal, Rabbi Jehiel, 149
Mikveh Yisra'el (Costa), 200
minyan, assembling a, 26–
  28
minyan ha-shetarot
  ("documentary
  reckoning"), 30
mishloah manot (gifts at
  Purim), 87
Mishnah
  on *afikoman*, 145
  annulment of vows, 42
  creation of, 193
  harvesting of omer, 181–
    182

Hebrew calendar, 29
January 1, 221
makban, 81
military metaphors, 17
plant-man, stories about,
  107–111
Shavu'ot, 213
tsholent documented in,
  5
Yom Kippur, description
  of, 39–40
Möllin, Rabbi Jacob, 63,
  212
Moose Jaw, Canada, 27
Mordecai, 127, 131–133
Moses
  dramatizations about,
    169–172
  in Islamic literature, 38–
    40
  Jonah, compared to, 46
Mother's Day, Jewish, 225–
  227
mourning
  for destruction of
    Temples, 230
  during Omer season,
    185–187
Muhammad, 37–41
Muharram, month of, 40
Muslim Caliphate, 194. *see
  also* Islam
mystical tradition. *see*
  Kabbalah

Nahmanides, 59
Nebuchadnezzar, King, 79, 125
Nehemiah, 192
New Brunswick, Canada, 28
New Testament, 56
new year, "civil," 221–224
Night (Wiesel), 19
Ninevites, repentance of, 45–47
Nisan, month of, 137–139
Nissim, of Gerona, 78
Noah, 138
noisemakers, at Purim, 118–119
Nöldecke, Theodor, 168
North American Jews. *see* Canada; United States

Old Testament, 68. *see also* Bible
Omer season, 179–184, 185–187
oral law *vs.* written scripture, 43, 183–184
oral tradition, of Islam, 38
oral tradition *vs.* written scripture, 56–57. *see also* Mishnah
Oriental Jewry, 88–89
orkhei hadayyanim (professional pleaders), 16

Orthodox Judaism, 122, 161–162, 210
Otto, Rudolf, 48–49
Oysher, Moishe, 153–155

paganism, 76, 85
Biblical misinterpretations, 222
feasts, 145
January 1, 224
Palestine
ancient tradition of, 25
Jewish population in, 193
Palestinian Talmud
creation of, 193
plant-man, stories about, 108, 110
on seder, 146
palm fronds as sign of victory, 17
Palm Sunday, 56–57
Pardo, David, 64
parodies of Purim, 115–119
parpisa, 20–21
Parthians, 96
Passover
anti-Semitism during, 166–168
dramatization of story, 169–172
Elijah tradition, 156–158
Exodus, 147–150
freedom, 151–152

gift traditions of, 87
Had Gadya, 153–155
Islamic interpretation of, 39
raisin-wine on, 159–162
Red Sea, parting of, 172, 173–175
seder compared to Roman banquet, 143–146
women's roles during, 77, 163–165
penitence. *see* Yom Kippur
Pentateuch, Purim references in the, 116
Pentecost, 214
Persia
    Hanukkah tradition in, 89
    Sassanian dynasty, 96
Persian Gulf, 175
Pesah. *see* Passover
Pfingsten, 214
Philo Judaeus, 147–148, 171–172, 174
philosophers, in Mishnah, 75
phoenix, legend of, 171
Pinhas of Koretz, 73
piyyutim. see poetry
plant-man, stories about, 107–111
plants on Shavu'ot, 212–214
Plato, 44–145, 75

poetry, 15
Akdamut, 215–218
Hoshanna hymns, 57
musical notation and, 206–207
for Omer season, 186
origins of, 23–25
Prince Rupert, Canada, 26–27
prohibition of alcohol in United States, 159–160
proselytising. *see* conversion
Protestant Reformation, 70, 121
Ptolemy Philadelphus, King, 181
Purim
    as astrological myth, 131–133
    carnival atmosphere of, 115–119
    gift traditions of, 87
    Hanukkah, compared to, 71–72
    resistance to holiday, 120–123
    women's roles during, 77
"Purim-Torah," 116

Qur'an, 38, 40

Rabbah, 117
Rachel, *yahrzeit* of, 225–227

rain, praying for, 101–103
Ramadan, Fast of, 37–41
rape, 78
Rashbam, 164
Rashi, 20, 78, 164
  on Passover wine
    tradition, 158
  on plant-man stories, 110
Rav, 222
Rava, 117
Rebecca, 225
Red Sea, 152, 172, 173–175,
    217–218
Reform Judaism, 122, 123,
    161–162, 210
Renaissance era, 31–32
Rohling, Augustus, 167–168
Rokeah, Rabbi Eleazar, 165
Roman Empire
  calendrical calculations
    of, 29
  Christianity and, 193
  feasts, 143–146
  Herod and, 90
  judicial system, 16
  Juvenal, 5
  Kalends, festival of the,
    221
  mythology, 223–224
  triumphal arches, 84
Rosenzweig, Franz, 49–51
Rosh Hashanah
  Hebrew calendar, 29–33
  judgment and, 56

minyan for, 26–28
Nisan compared to, 137
observing for two days,
    208
poetry during, 23–25
Shavu'ot, compared to,
    213
Tashlikh ceremony, 20–22
Rosh Hodesh observance,
    226
Roth, Cecil, 229–230
Ruth, Book of, 205

Sabbath
  angels and, 9–11
  candles for, 6–8, 94–97
  cooking on, 3–5
  as festival, 181
  fire, prohibitions
    regarding, 62–63
  Hanukkah candles,
    compared to, 72
  Omer season
    significance, 180
  Vashti and, 125
Sadah festival, 96
Safed tradition for *Tashlikh*
    ceremony, 21
Saint John, Canada, 28
Samaritans, 91–93
Samson of Sens, 108–109
Samuel of Falaise, 164
sanegoros (prosecuting
    attorney), 16–19

Sanhedrin, 181
Sarah, 225
Saskatchewan, Canada, 27
Satan, 21, 39–40
Saudi Arabia, 175
sawm (fast), 38
Scheiber, Alexander, 200
Schreiber, Rabbi Moses, 210
Scroll of Esther. *see*
   Megillah
Sea of Reeds, 173–175
Second Commonwealth,
   137
Second Temple, 81, 191. *see*
   also First Temple
   Baitusim, 180–183
   date of destruction, 229–
      230
   era, 137–139
   Omer season observance,
      179–180
   Purim and, 115, 116
seder
   Elijah tradition, 156–158
   Last Supper, 160
   leaning during, 163–165
Seder 'Olam (Order of the
   World), 30–33
Sefer HaQabbalah (Ibn
   Daud), 31
Seleucid era, 30–33, 80
selichot service, 18
separation of Church and
   State, 161–162

Sephardim
   Akdamut recitation, 215–
      218
   Hanukkah traditions of,
      88–90
   La'g Ba'omer tradition,
      186
   origin of, 218
   raisin-wine and, 160
   Sabbath candles, 7
Septuagint, 68
   Red Sea, 173
   Sabbath as festival, 181
Serapis cult, 222
Shabbat. *see* Sabbath
Shabbetai Zvi, 10, 88
Shaharit service, 24
Shalom, Rabbi Abraham,
   132
Shalom Aleikhem hymn, 10
shalom bayit (domestic
   peace), 6
shamash candle, 7
Shapira, Rabbi Elia, 64
Shavu'ot, 179
   Akdamut, recitation of,
      215–218
   decorating with greenery,
      212–214
   divorce and, 208–211
   Obadiah the Proselyte,
      205–207
sheaves, wave-offering of.
   see Omer season

Shechem, 79
She'iltot talmudic code,
163–164
shekels, equality of Jews
and, 138
Shelomah Yitzhaki. see
Rashi
Shema prayer, 24
Shemini 'Atzeret, 62
Sherira, Rabbi, 30
Shevat, fifteenth of, 107–
111
Shiite Muslim beliefs, 40
Shulhan 'Arukh (Karo), 32,
60
on "barnacle goose," 109
greenery on Shavu'ot,
212
La'g Ba'omer tradition,
186
Siddur, calendrical
calculations in, 101–
103
Simeon, 78–79
Simhat Torah, 61–64
Sin, house of, 182–183
sins, casting of, 20–22
Sirkes, Rabbi Joel, 71
Sisera, 79
slavery, in Egypt, 151–152
solar calendar, 102–103,
182
Solomon, King, 201

Song of Songs, 213
Sophocles, 75
Spanish Inquisition, 4–5,
127–130
Star of Redemption
(Rosenzweig), 50
State, separation of Church
and, 161–162
State of Israel (modern)
Hebrew calendar in, 101
seal, official, 84
Stoicism, 171–172
Strack, Hermann, 168
Sukkot, 17
Hosanna ritual, 55–57
Hoshana Rabbah
moonlight,
superstition about,
58–60
Simhat Torah, 61–64
summer fruit, first offering
of, 213
superstition. see also
Kabbalah
about plant-man, 107–
111
about Tashlikh ceremony,
21–22
astrological
interpretation of
Purim, 131–133
Hoshana Rabbah
moonlight, 58–60

symbolism ·
  of calendrical
    calculations, 29–33
  of Exodus, 147–150
  of Menorah, 83–86
  of seder, 143–146
  of shadows in moonlight,
    59–60
  of *Tashlikh* ceremony,
    21–22
"Symposium" (Plato), 144–
  145
synagogues
  decorating, 212–214
  venues for, 27
Syrian Church, 47

Tabernacle, inauguration of
  the, 138
Tachanun prayers, 138
Talmud. *see also*
  Babylonian Talmud
  angels, 9
  annulment of vows, 42
  Books of Maccabees, 69–
    70
  calendrical calculations
    of, 102
  drunkenness on Purim,
    117
  Greek references in, 74–76
  on leaning leftward at
    seder, 144

light, significance of, 72
Magi, references to, 96
Sabbath prohibitions, 4
tsholent documented in, 5
Vashti, references to, 126
Vilna printings, 166
Talmudjude, Der (Rohling),
  167–168
Tarfon, Rabbi, 157–158
Targum, 216–218
Tashlikh ceremony, 20–22
Temperance Movement,
  159–162
Temple. *see* First Temple;
  Second Temple
Temple Scroll, 137, 183
Ten tal umatar calendar
  formula, 101–103
Tiferet Israel (Lifschutz),
  109–110
Torah
  Akdamut, 215–218
  Hanukkah tradition
    linked to, 89
  Hoshana Rabbah, rituals
    of, 56
  humanity of the enemy,
    recognizing, 152
  light, significance of, 72
  Nisan, 137–139
  Omer season procedure,
    179
  reading of, 24

Torah (*continued*)
  revelation of, 212–214
  Sabbath prohibitions, 4
  Simhat Torah
    celebration, 61–64
  613 commandments of,
    43
  Stoicism and, 172
trees on Shavu'ot, 212–214
"Trial of God, The"
  (Wiesel), 19
tsholent, 3–5
Turgemans, 217
Turkey, traditions in, 63
two brothers, tale of, 199–
  201
tzom (fast), 38

United States Jewry
  Hanukkah,
    commercialization
      of, 87–89
  raisin-wine at Passover,
    159–162
Untanneh Tokef prayer, 17

Vashti, Queen, 116
  Christian views on, 121
  as feminist heroine, 124–
    126
Venice, *Akdamut*
  controversy in, 215
venues for synagogues, 27
Victoria, Canada, 26–28

Vilna edition of Talmud,
  166
Voltaire, 70
vows, annulment of, 42–44

werewolves superstition,
  111
wickedness, Philo Judaeus
  on, 148
Wiesel, Elie, 19
wine, fifth cup at seder,
  157–158
Winnipeg, Canada, 26–28
winter, 101–103, 222–223
women, roles in Judaism
  among Marranos, 129–
    130
  feminism, 124–126
  during Hanukkah, 77–79
  during Passover, 163–165
written law, oral law *vs.*, 43

Yadin, Yigael, 183
Yadua (animal), 108
Yannai, 24–25
Yemenite traditions, 30
  at Hanukkah, 89
  at Passover, 158
*Yetzer ha-tov vs. Yetzer ha-
  ra* (good *vs.* evil), 9
Yiddish, 154
Yitzhak, Rabbi Levi, 18–19
Yitzhaki, Shelomah. *see*
  Rashi

Yohanan, Rabbi, 223–224
Yom Kippur, 56
  Book of Jonah, 45–47
  Hoshana Rabbah and,
    58–60
  Islamic interpretation of,
    37–41, 39
  Kol Nidré and, 42–44
  minyan for, 26–28
  transformation of people
    during, 48–51

Yosippon legend, 81
Yukon, Canada, 27

Zera, Rabbi, 117
Zionist movement, 191–
    195, 195
Zipporah, 170
Zodiac, 131–133
Zohar, 58, 149
Zoroastrian Mazdean
    priesthood. *see* Magi

About the Author

Professor Eliezer Segal is currently serving as Head of the Department of Religious Studies at the University of Calgary, holding a Ph.D. in Talmud from the Hebrew University of Jerusalem. In addition to his scholarly articles and monographs on talmudic and midrashic literature (including the three-volume *The Babylonian Esther Midrash: A Critical Commentary*), he has published extensively for non-specialist audiences on diverse topics related to Jewish history and tradition, through his popular newspaper columns and his Web site. A collection of his articles, *Why Didn't I Learn This in Hebrew School?* was published in 1999 by Jason Aronson. His children's book, *Uncle Eli's Passover Haggadah*, a rhymed version of the traditional Passover night liturgy, has been a phenomenal success in digital and printed forms, and a sequel for Rosh Hashanah and Yom Kippur (*Uncle Eli Repents*) is in the works. Professor Segal has been involved in many inter-religious activities, and participated in comparative projects offering Jewish perspectives on such topics as: afterlife beliefs, scripture and oral tradition, and reforms of the criminal justice system.

Professor Segal resides in the western Canadian city of Calgary with his wife, Agnes, and his three sons, Yannai, Hananel, and Akiva.